ADULT COLORING BOOK

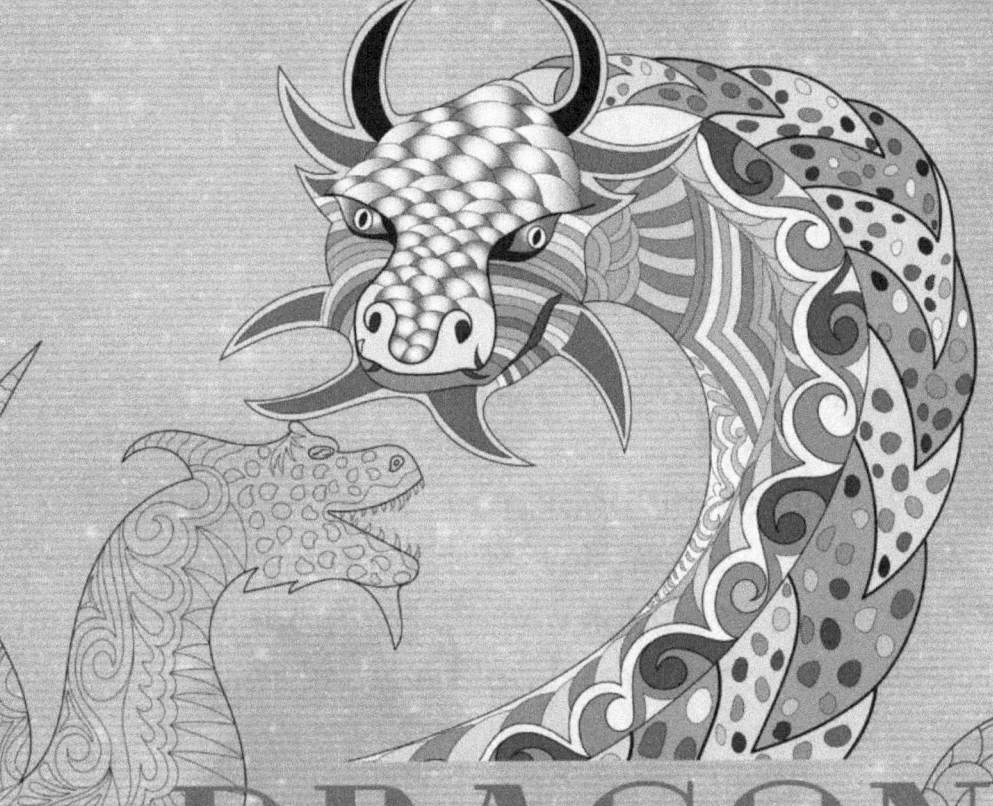

30 DESIGNS

DRAGONS

RELAX. COLOR. DE-STRESS.

Copyright © 2020 by Expression Press

All rights reserved. No part of this book may be reproduced or used in any manner without written permission of the copyright owner except for the use of quotations in a book review. For more information, address: expressionpressbooks@gmail.com

FIRST EDITION

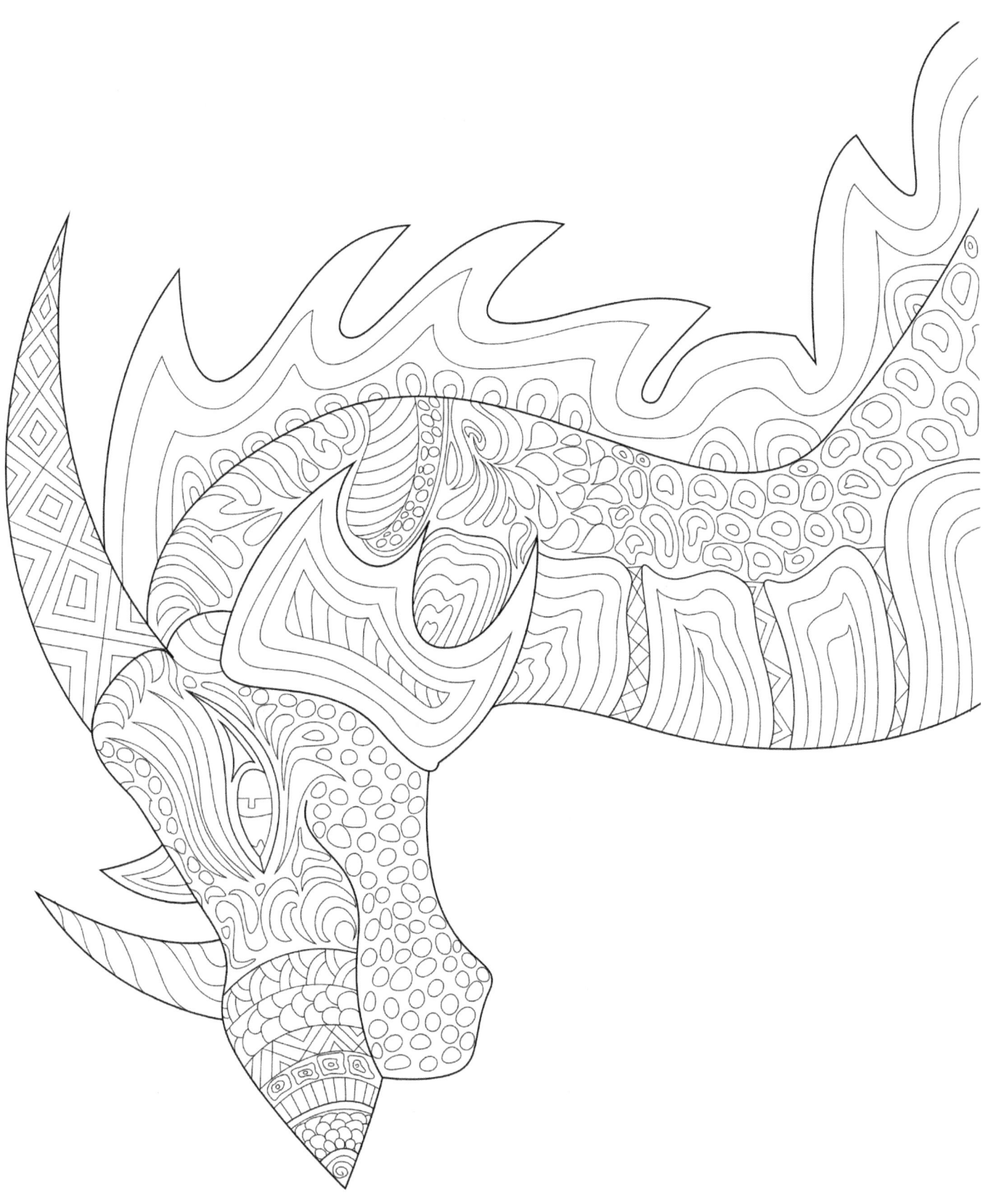

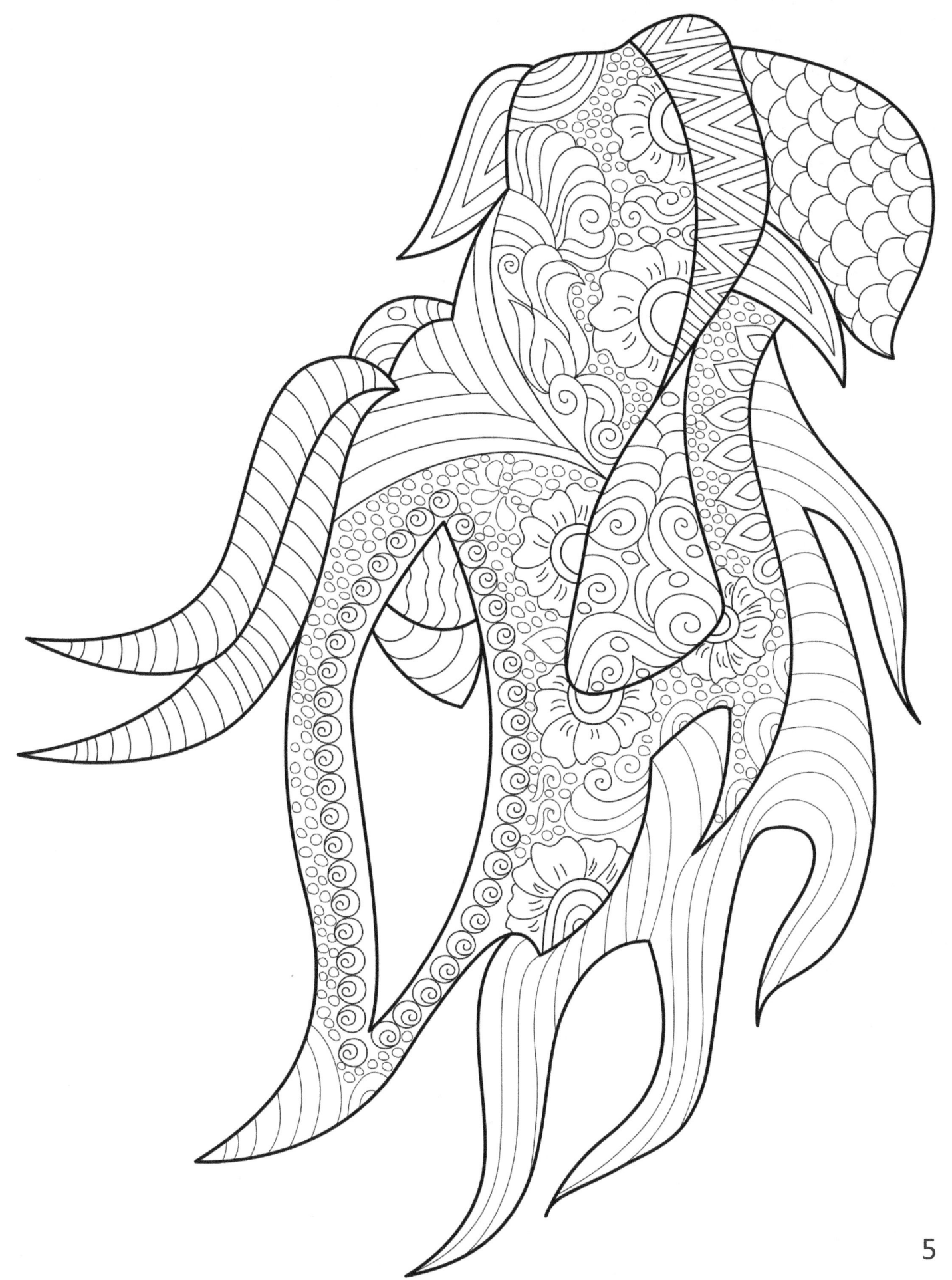

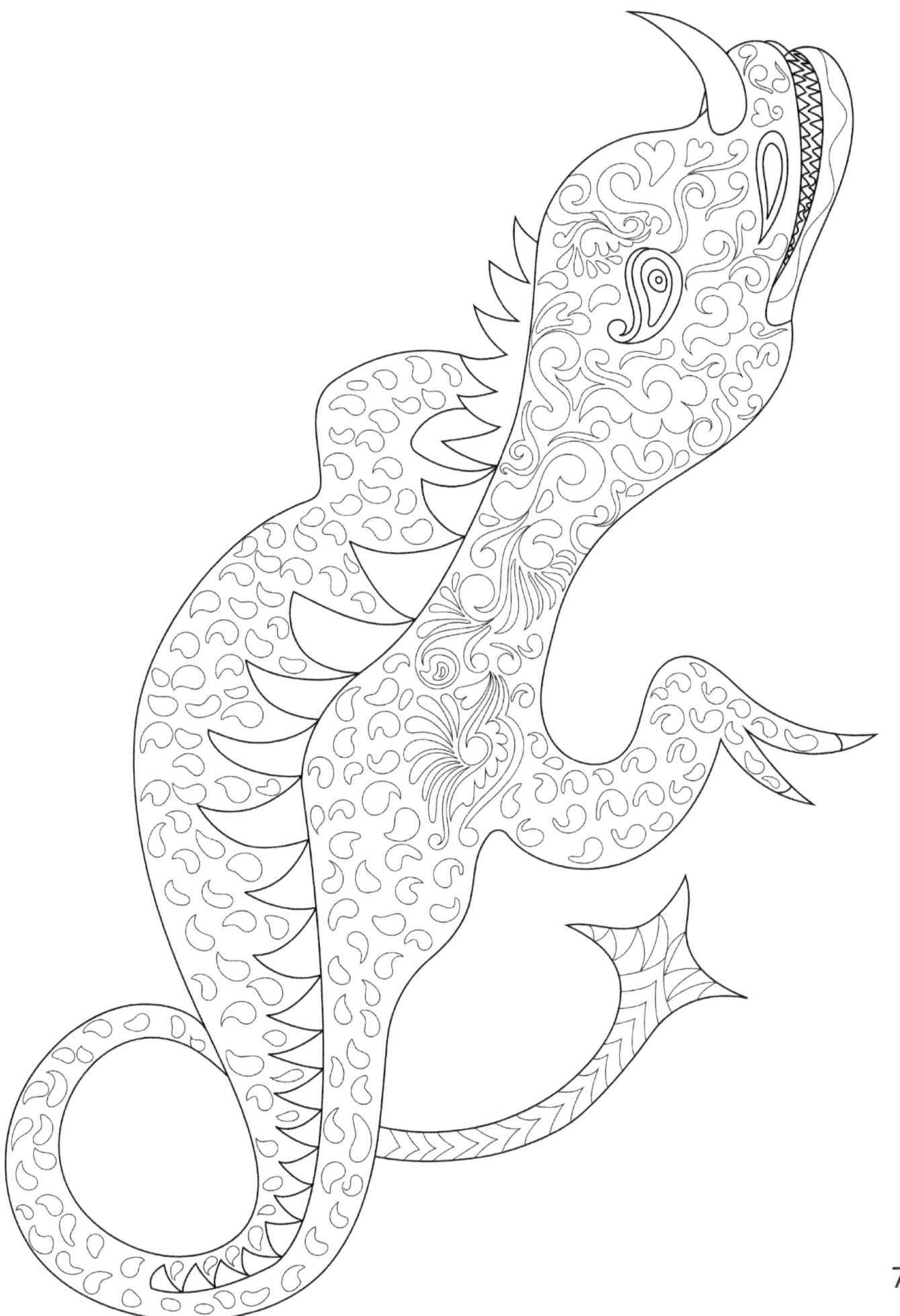

8

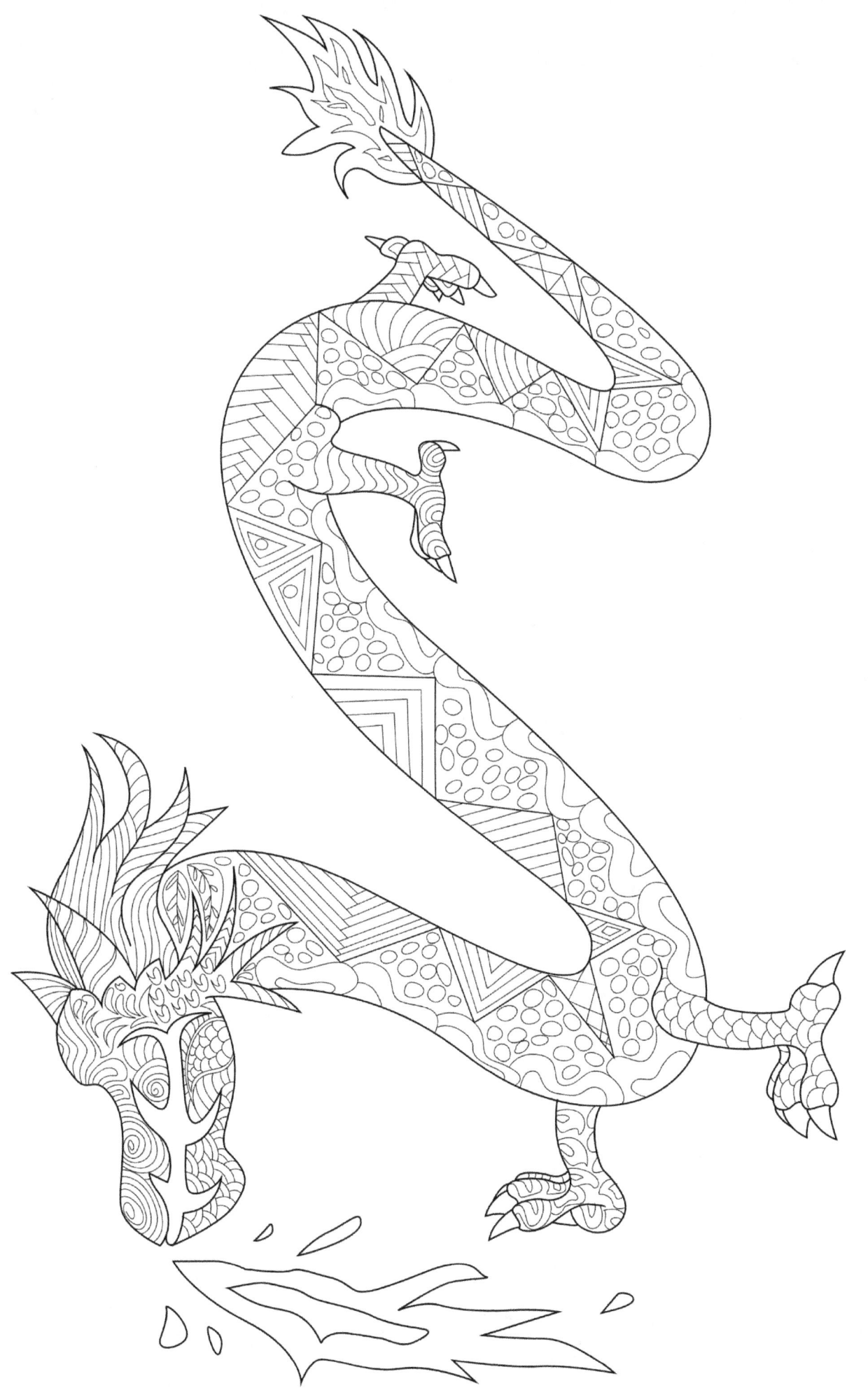

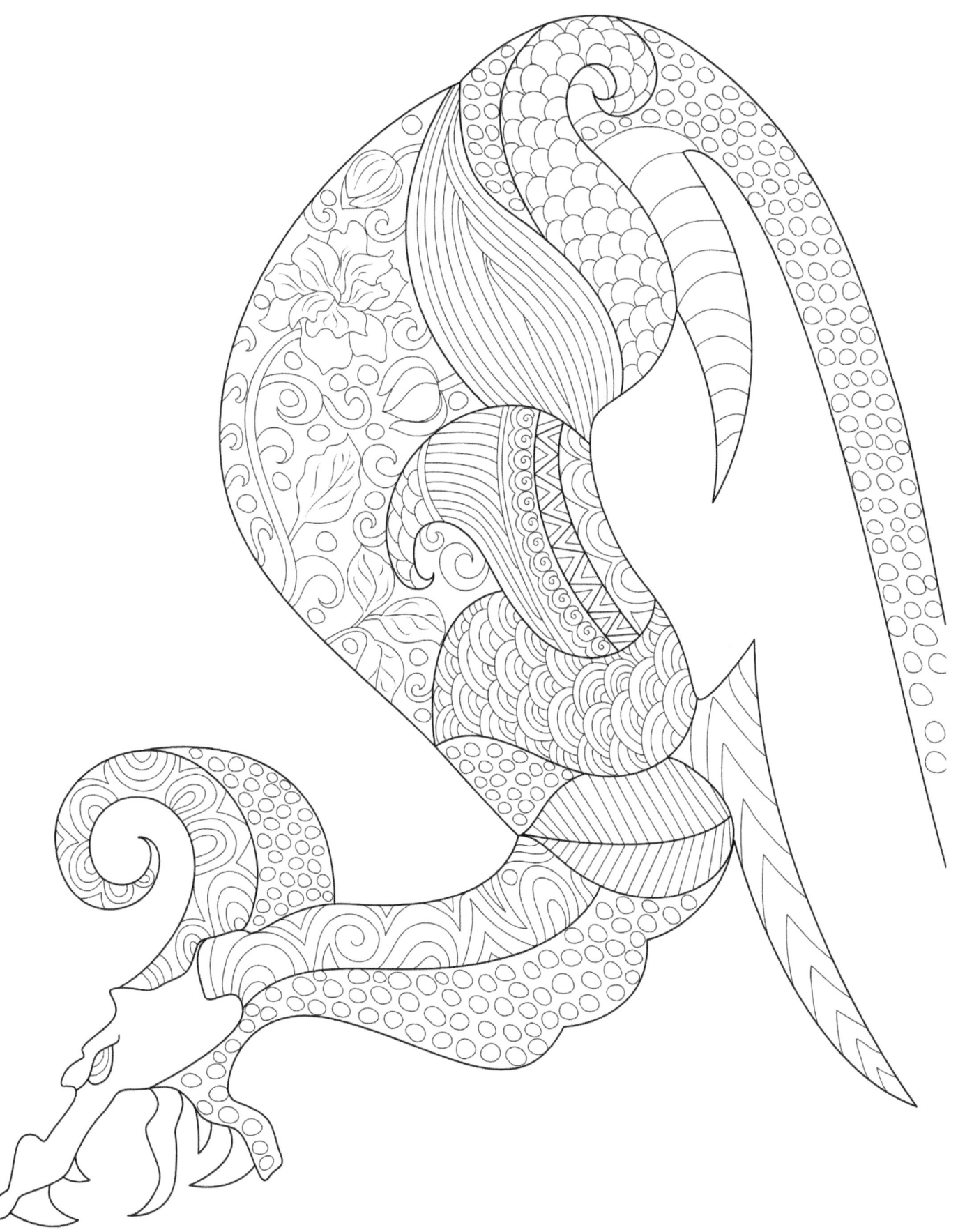

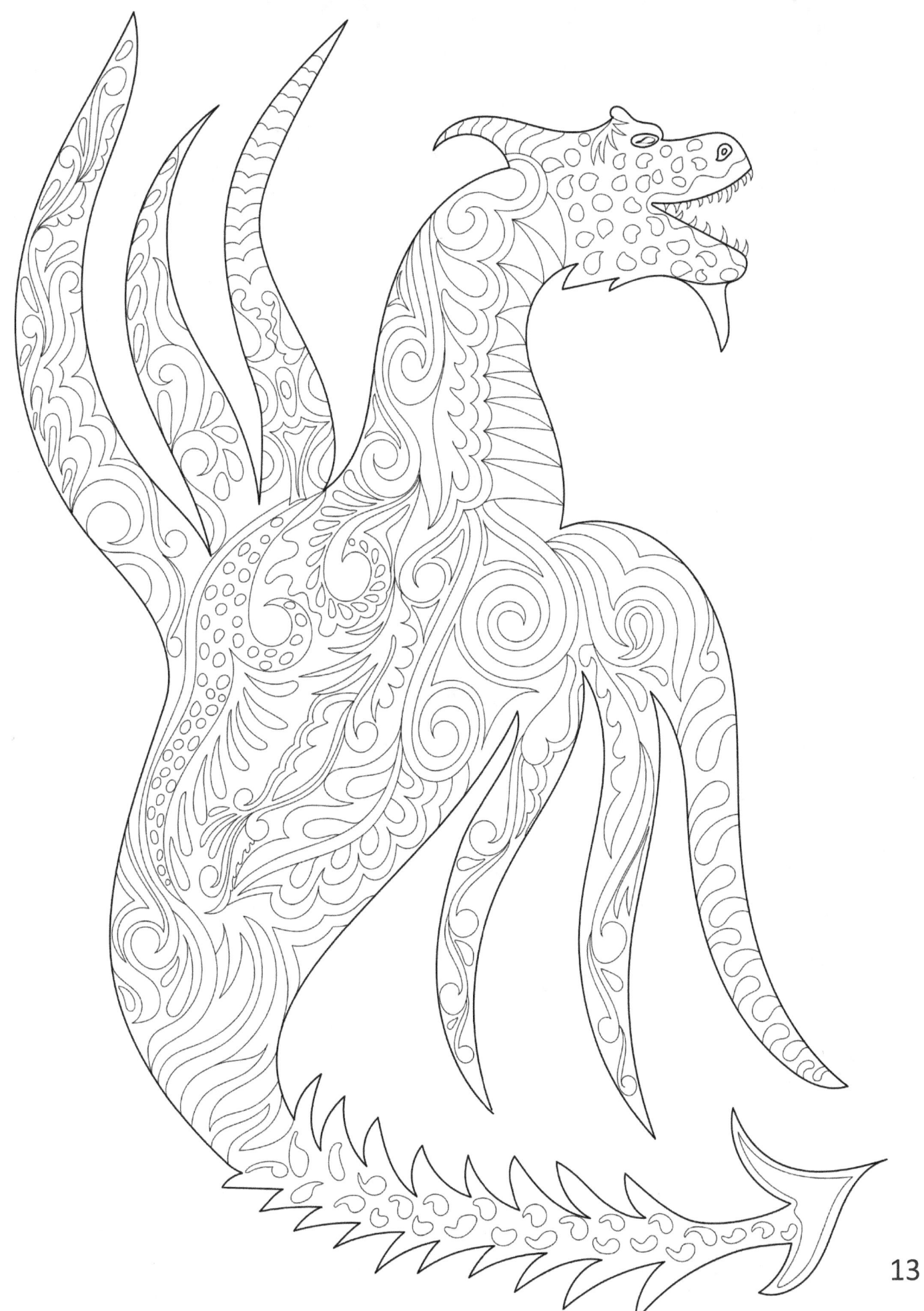

14

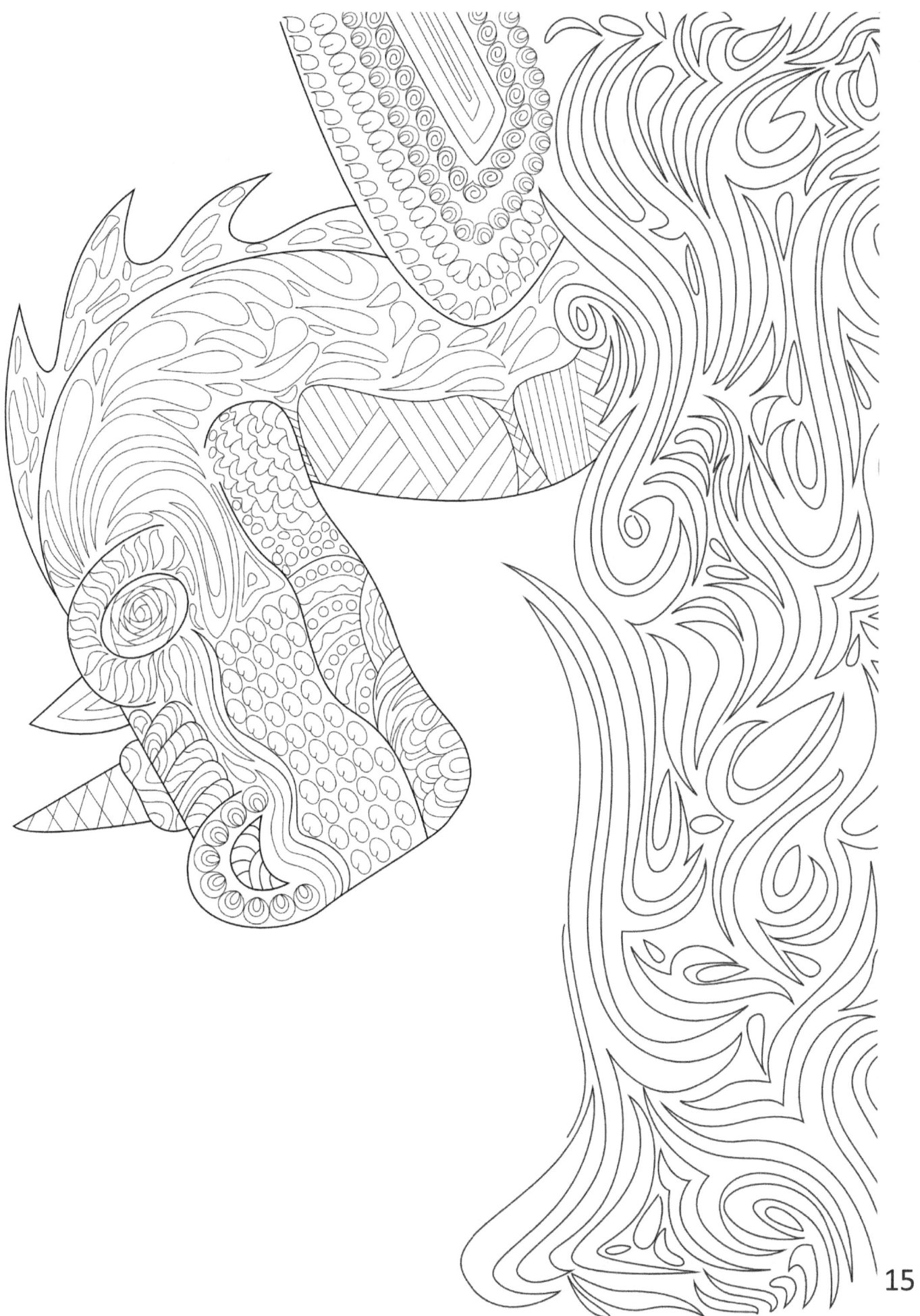

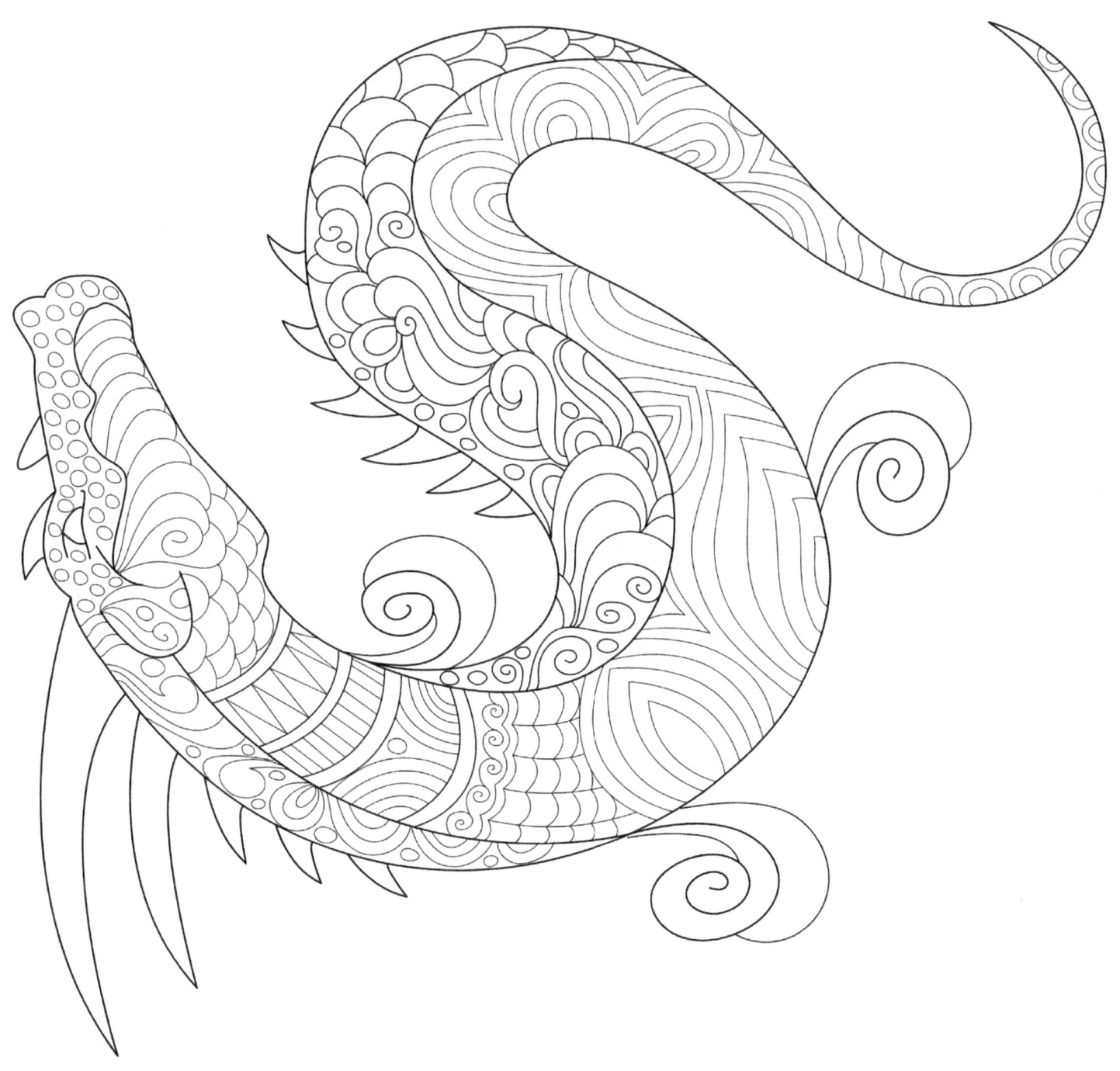

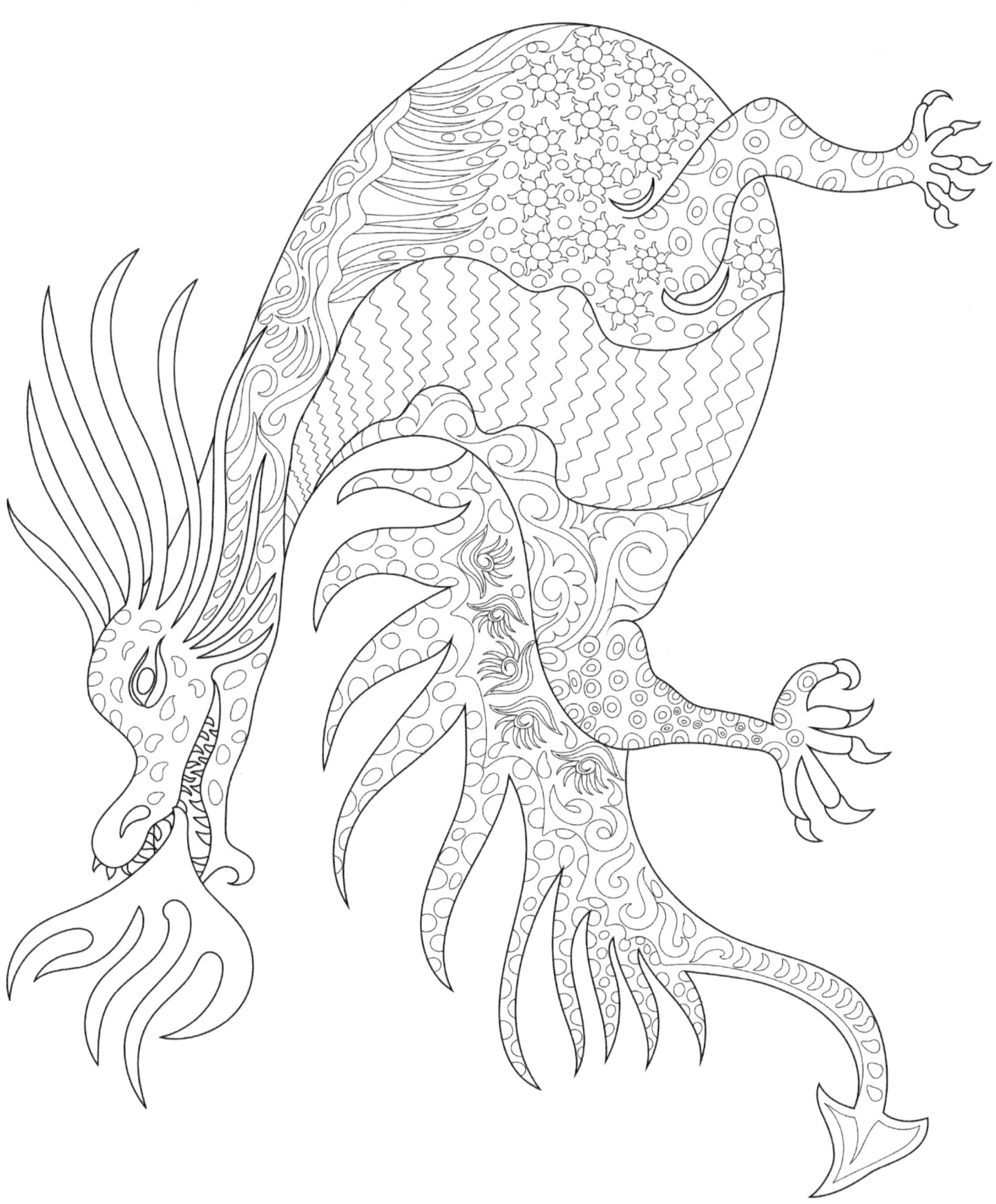

20

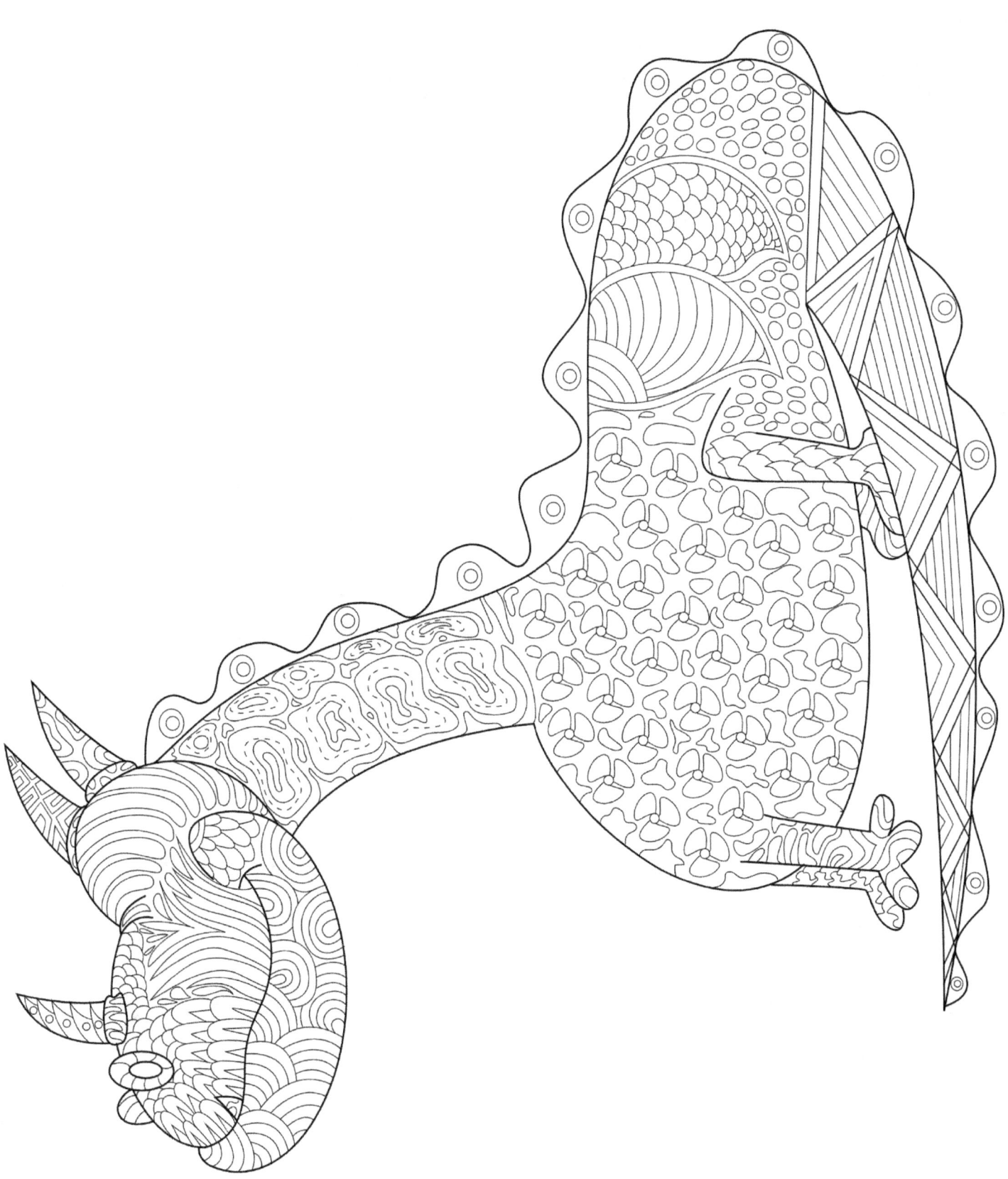

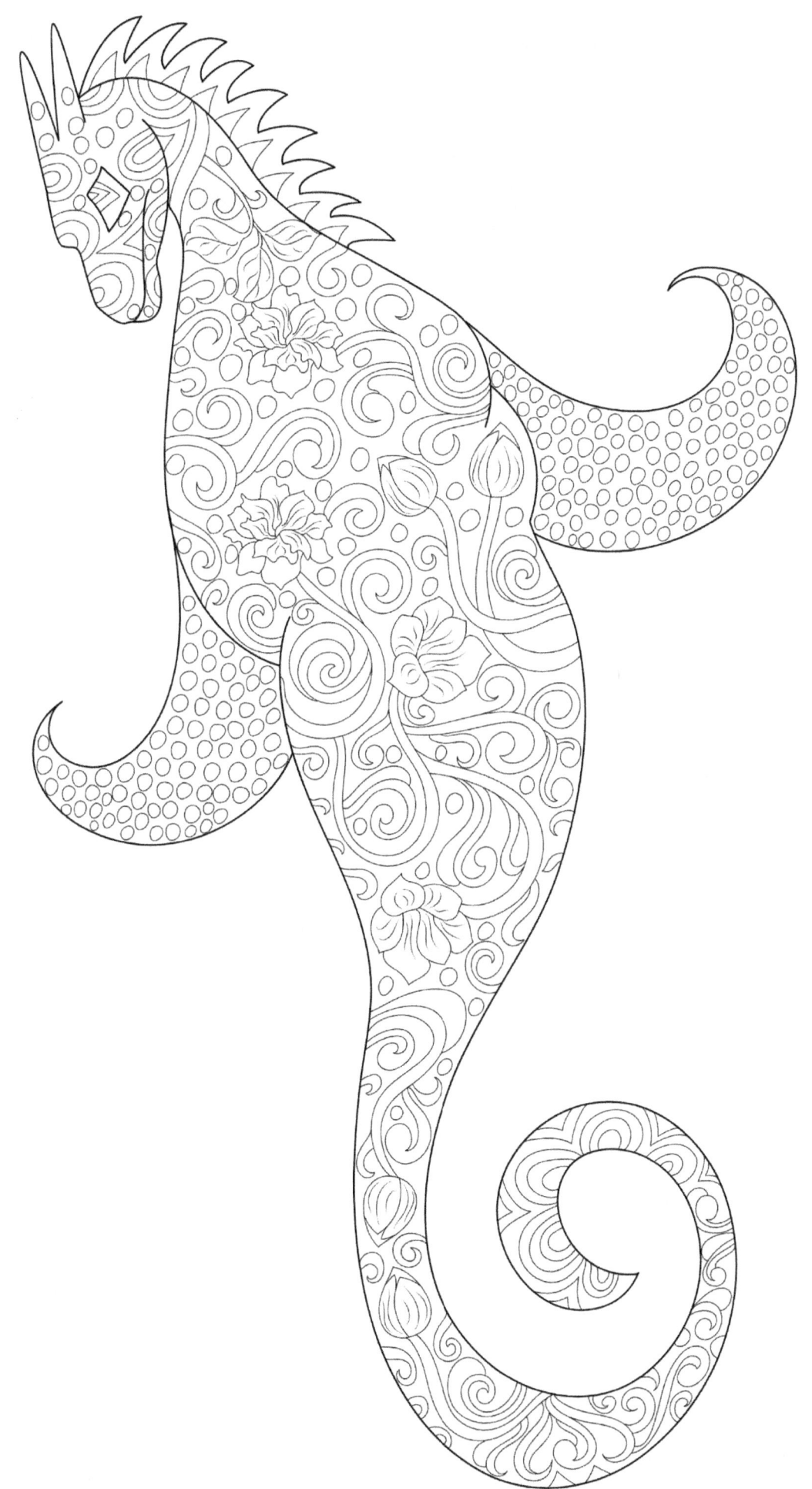

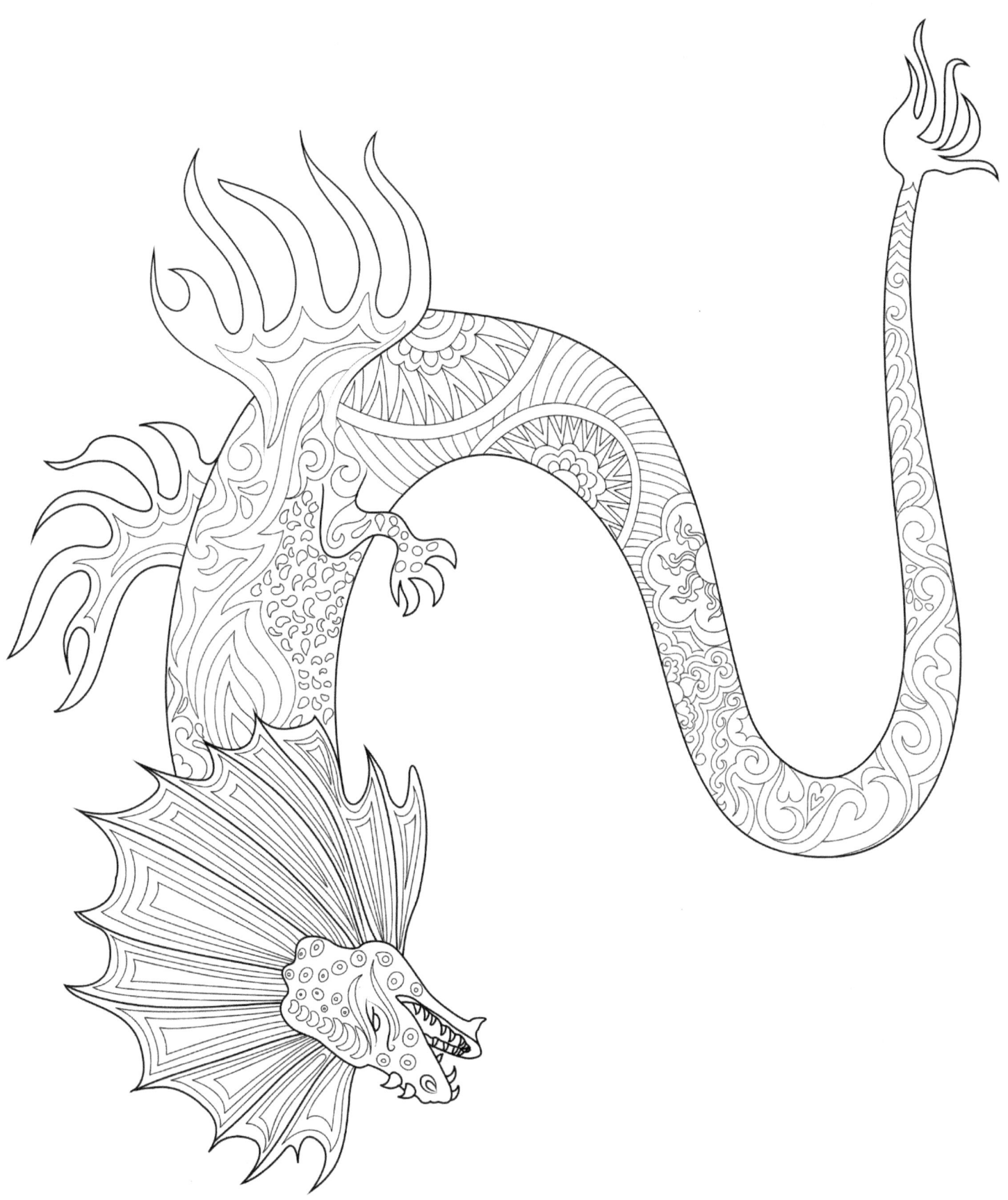

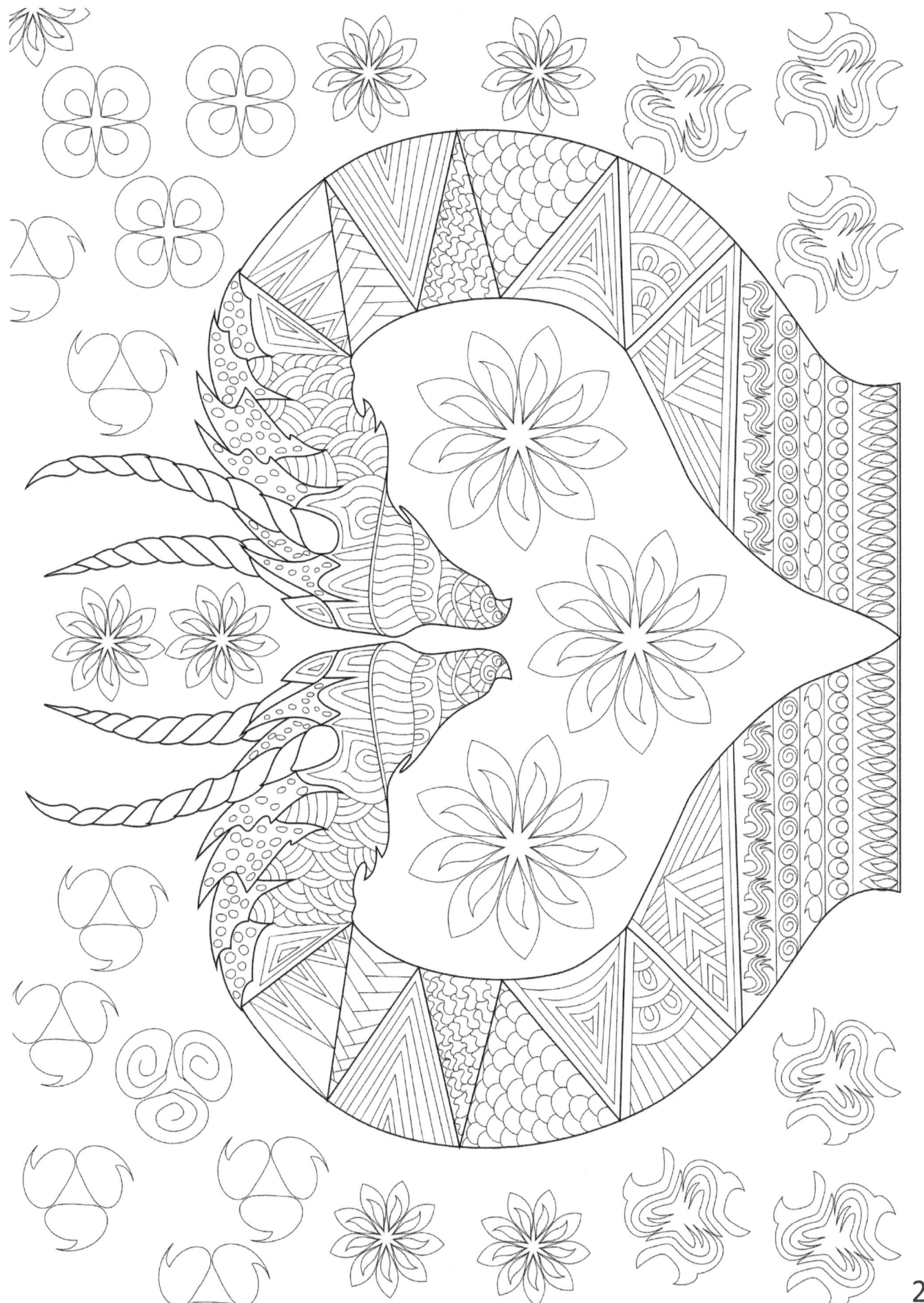

28

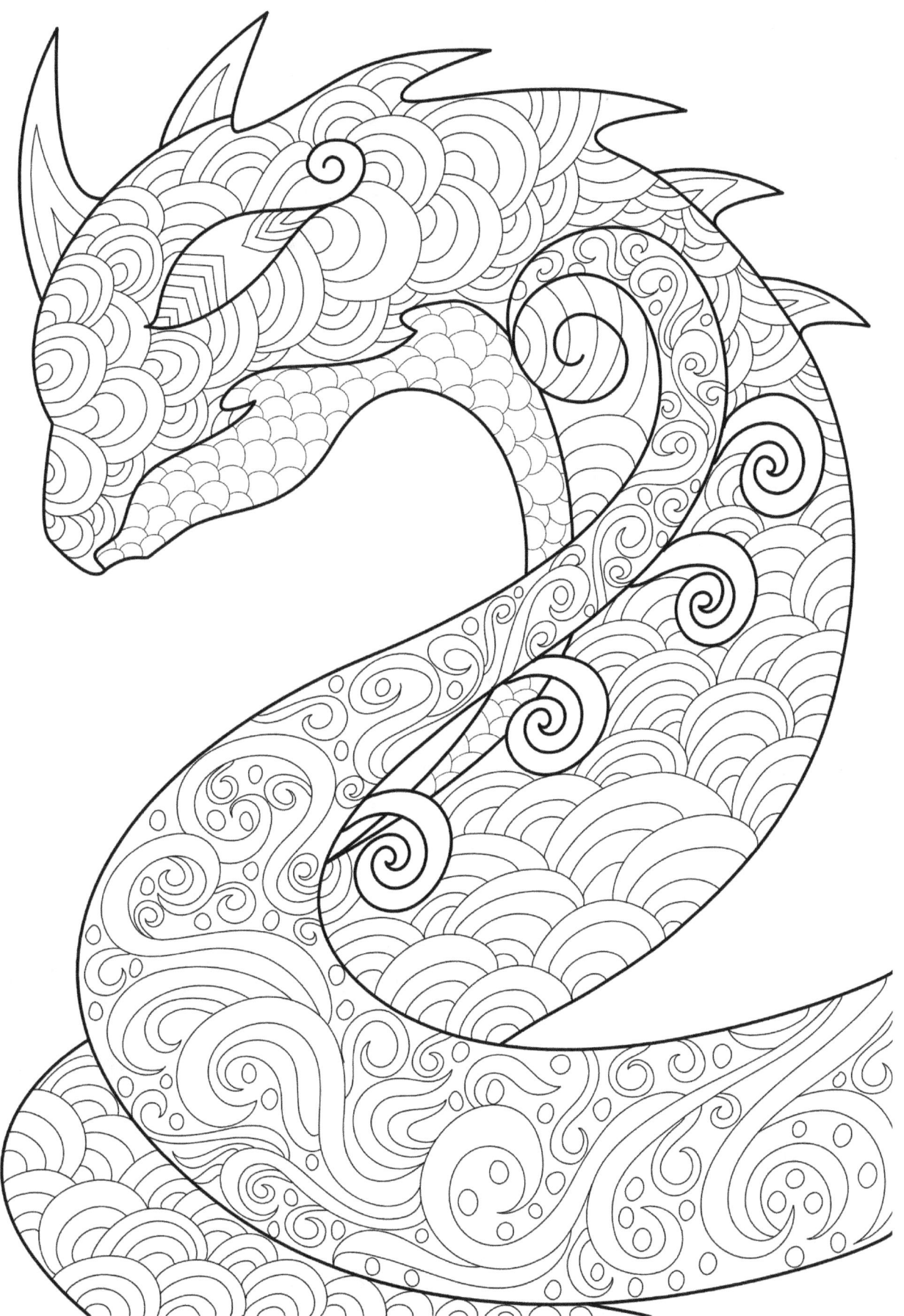

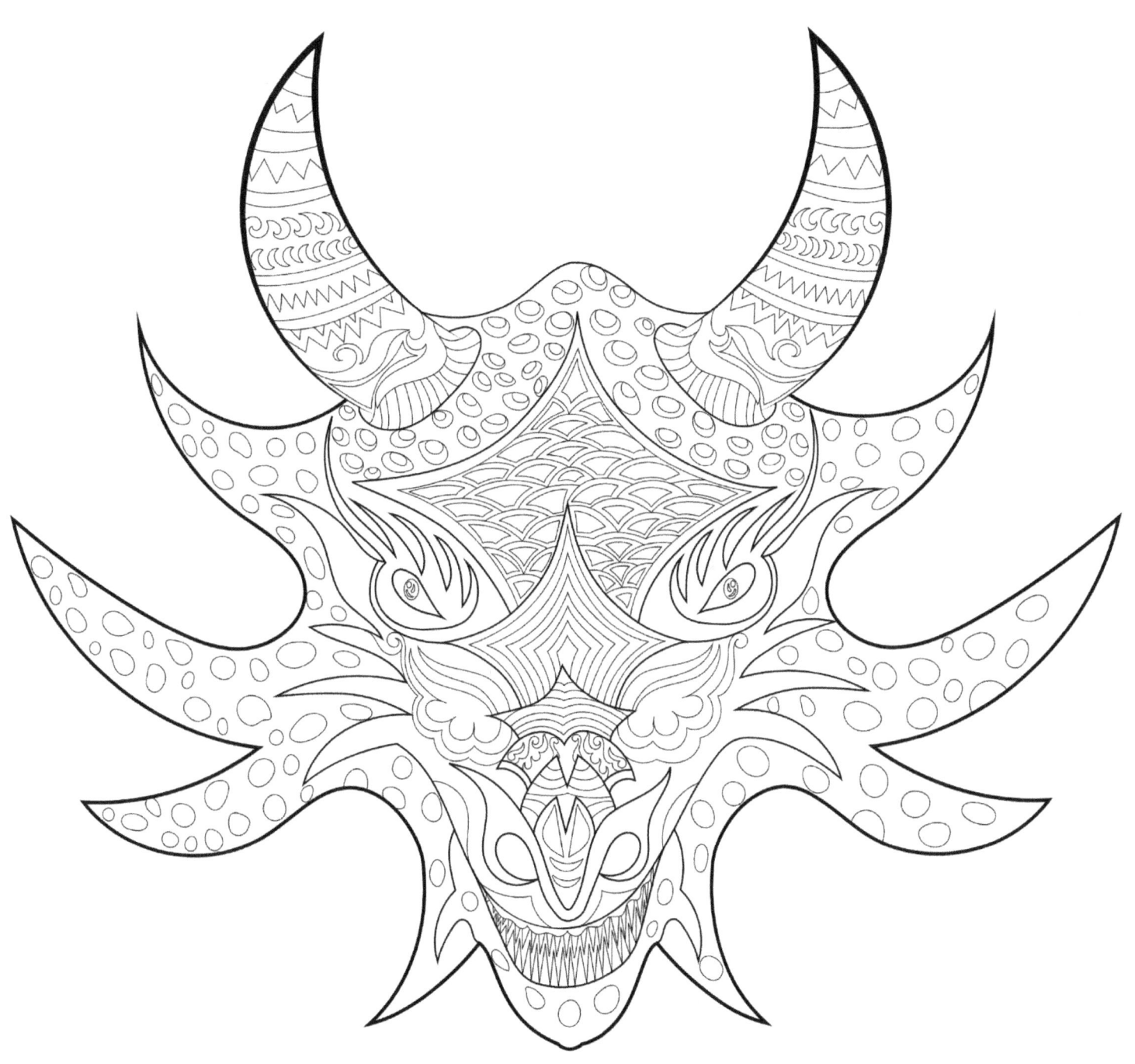

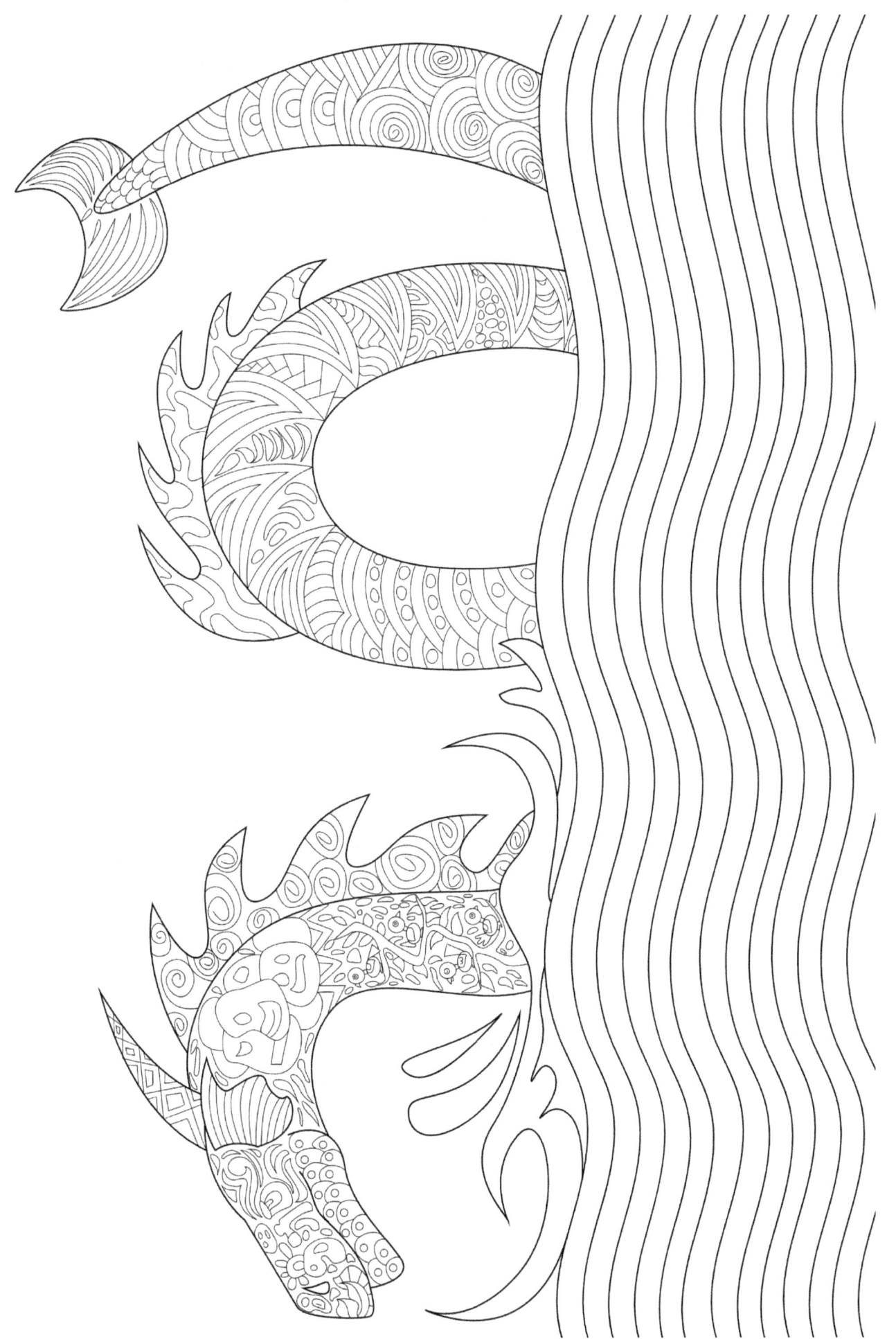

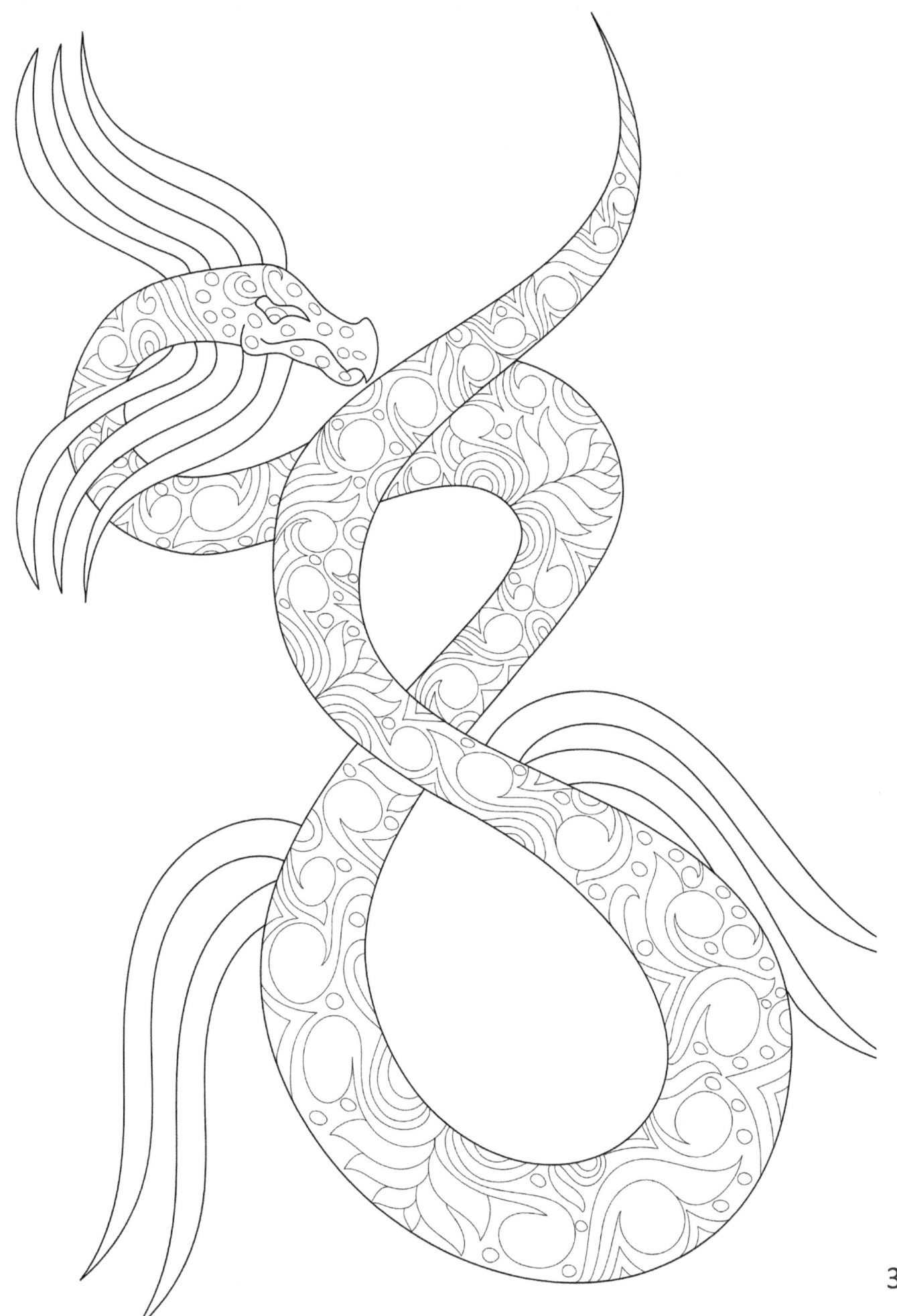

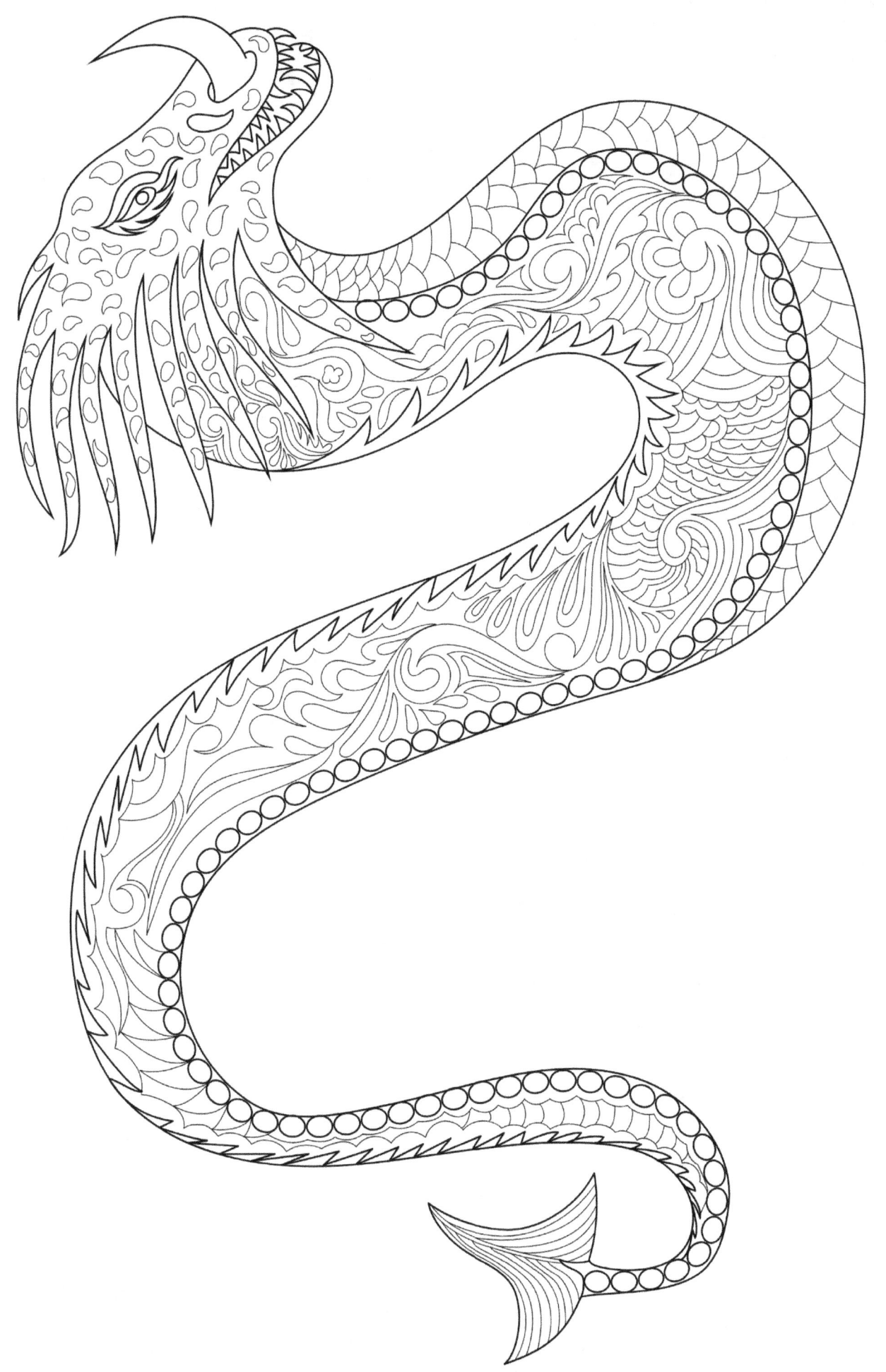

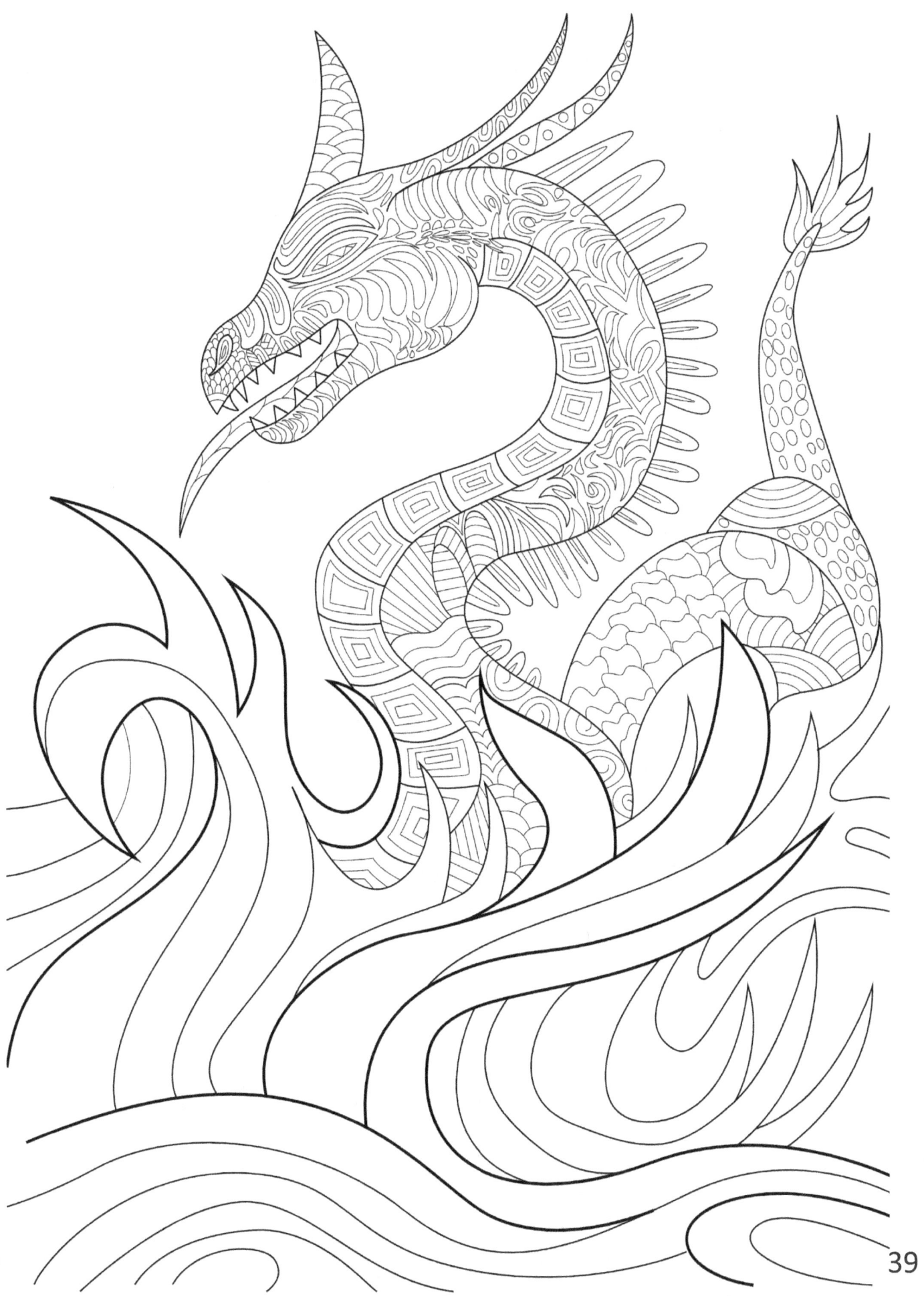

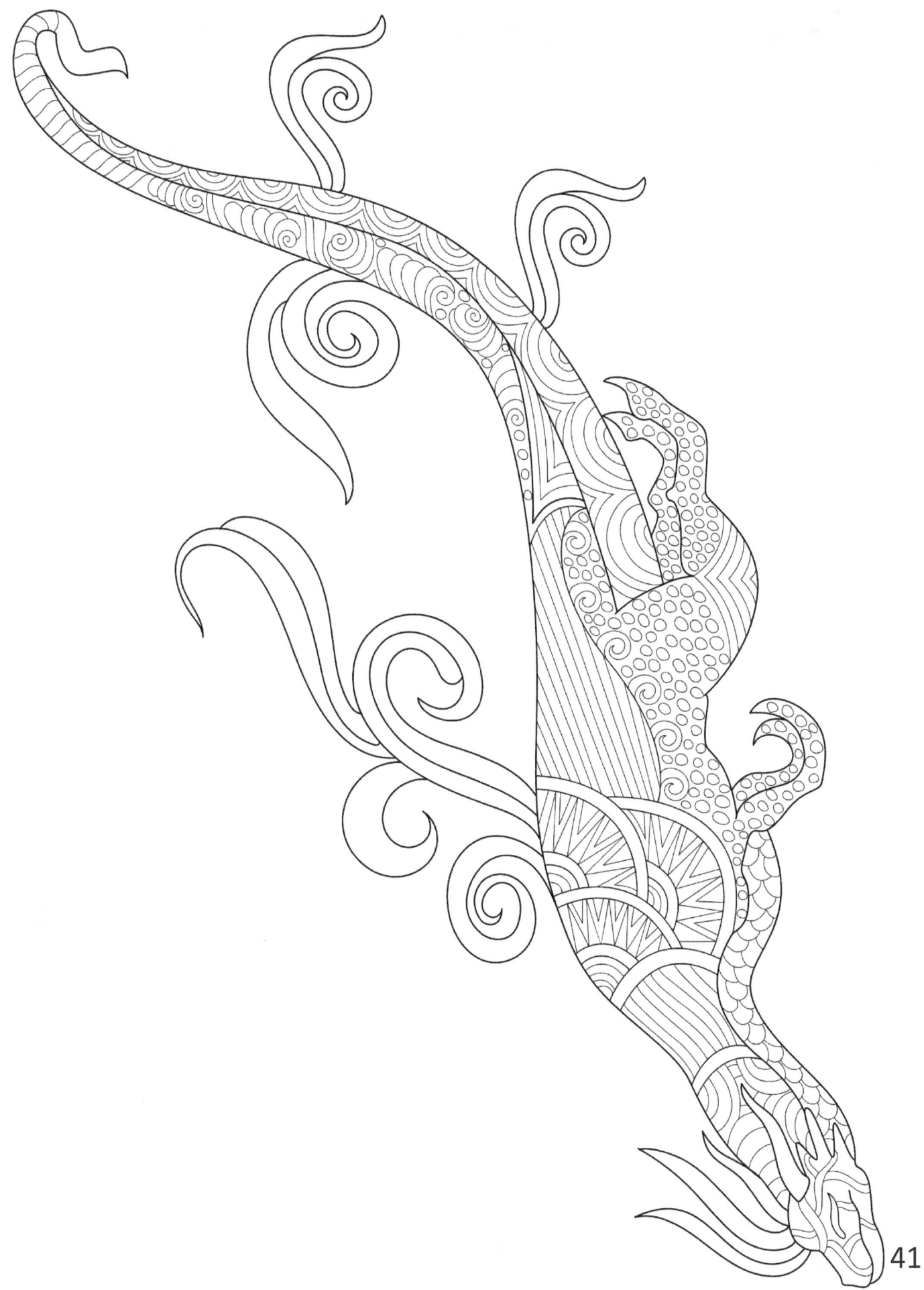

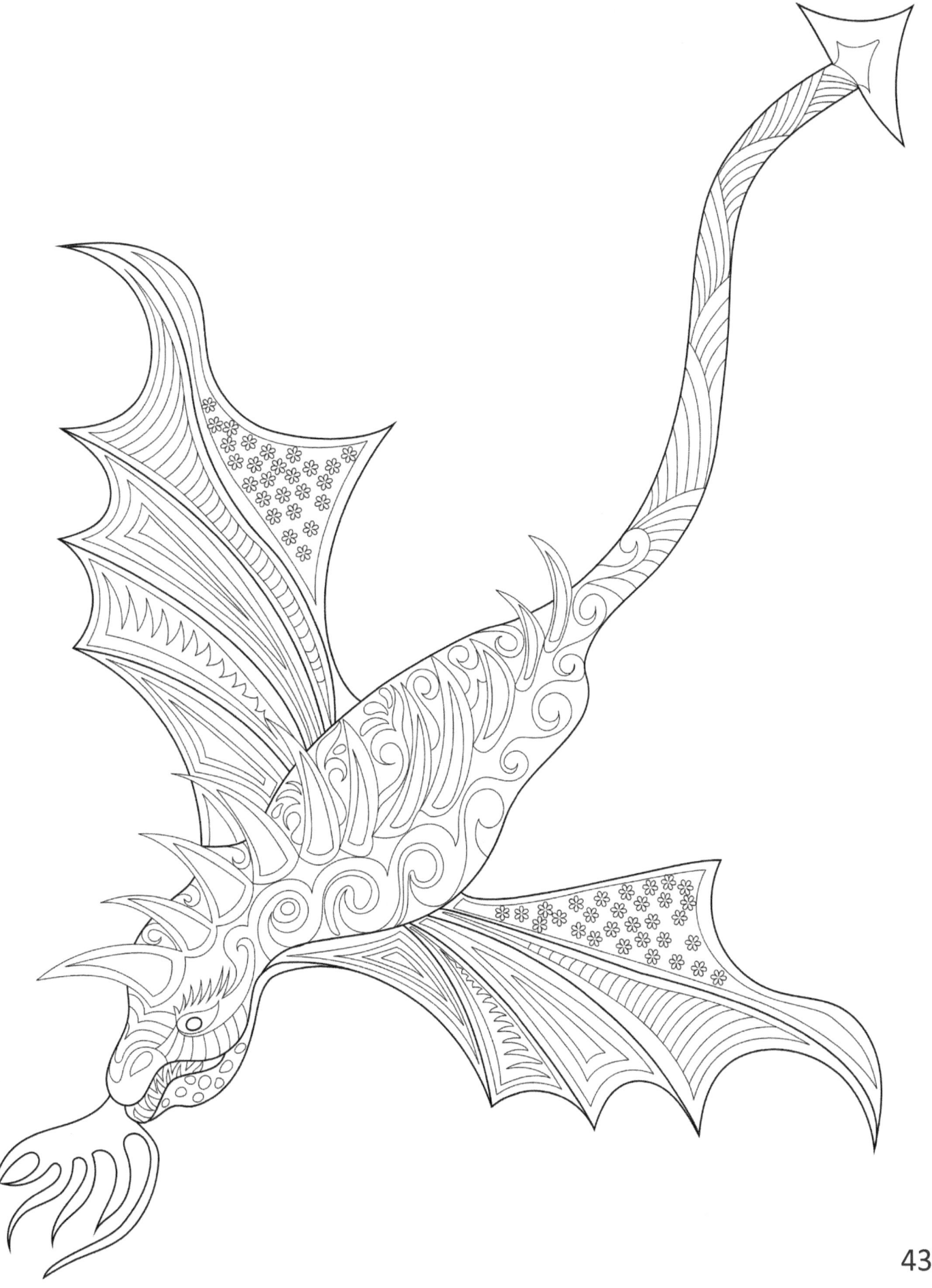

44

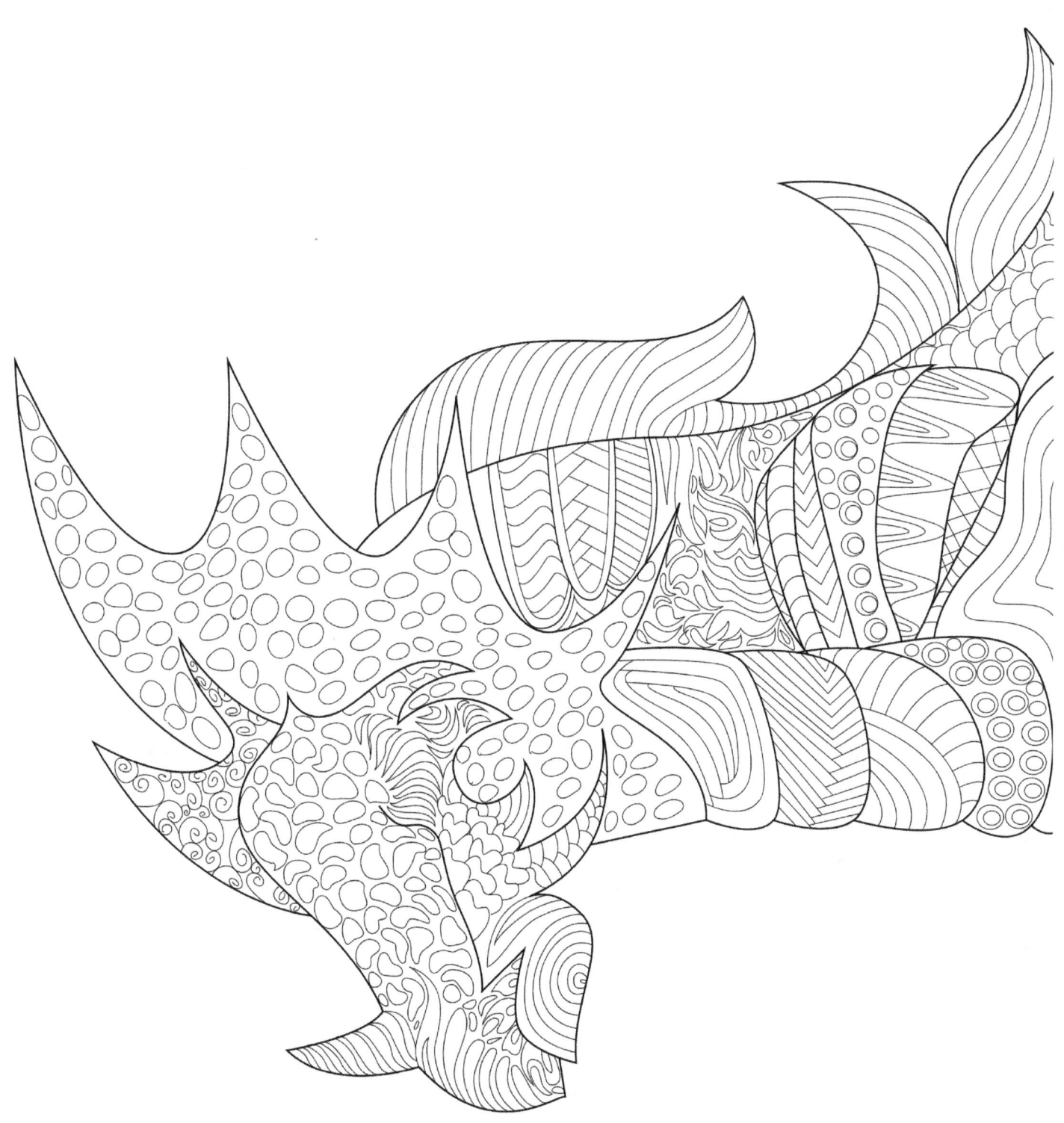

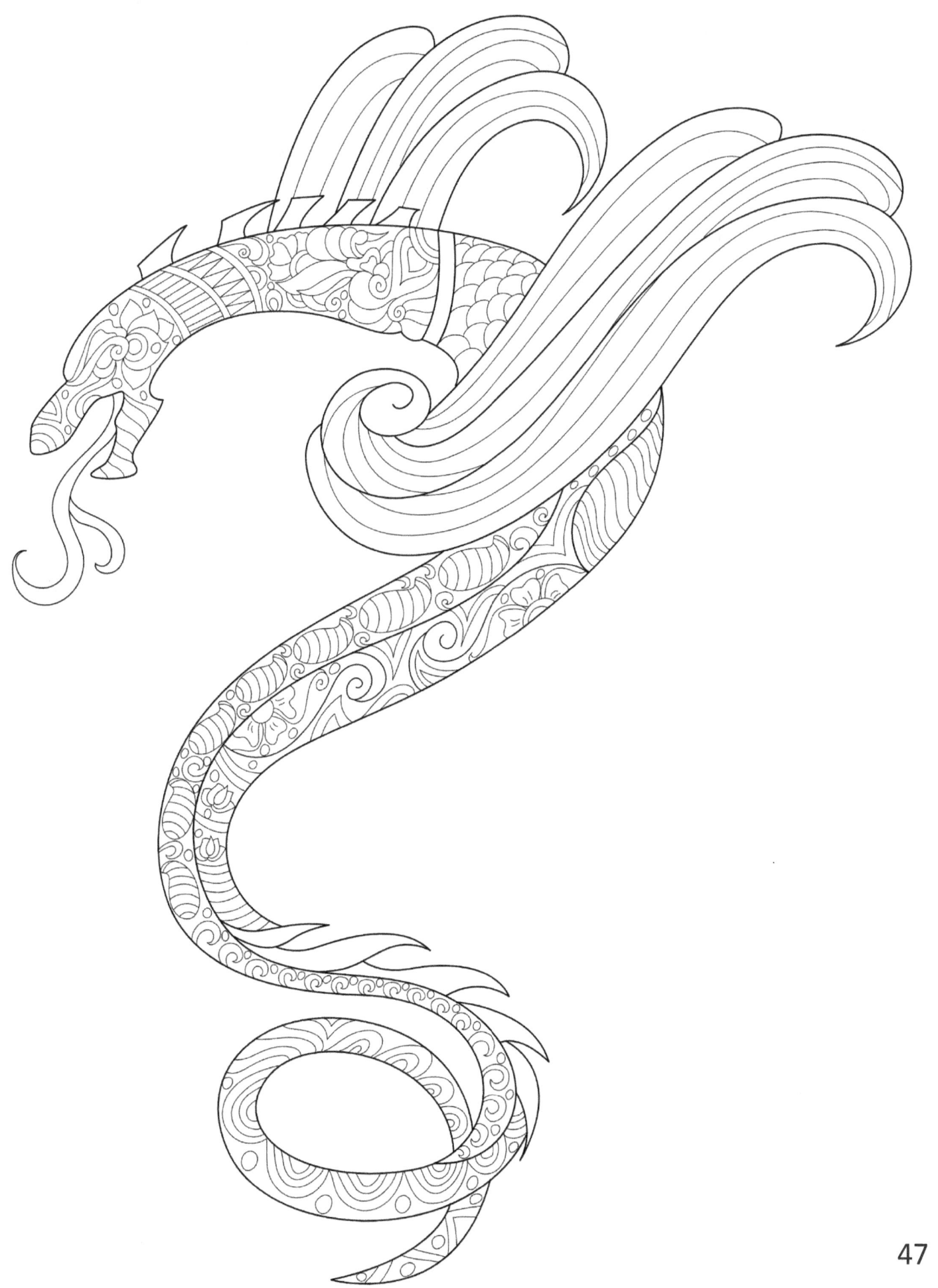

48

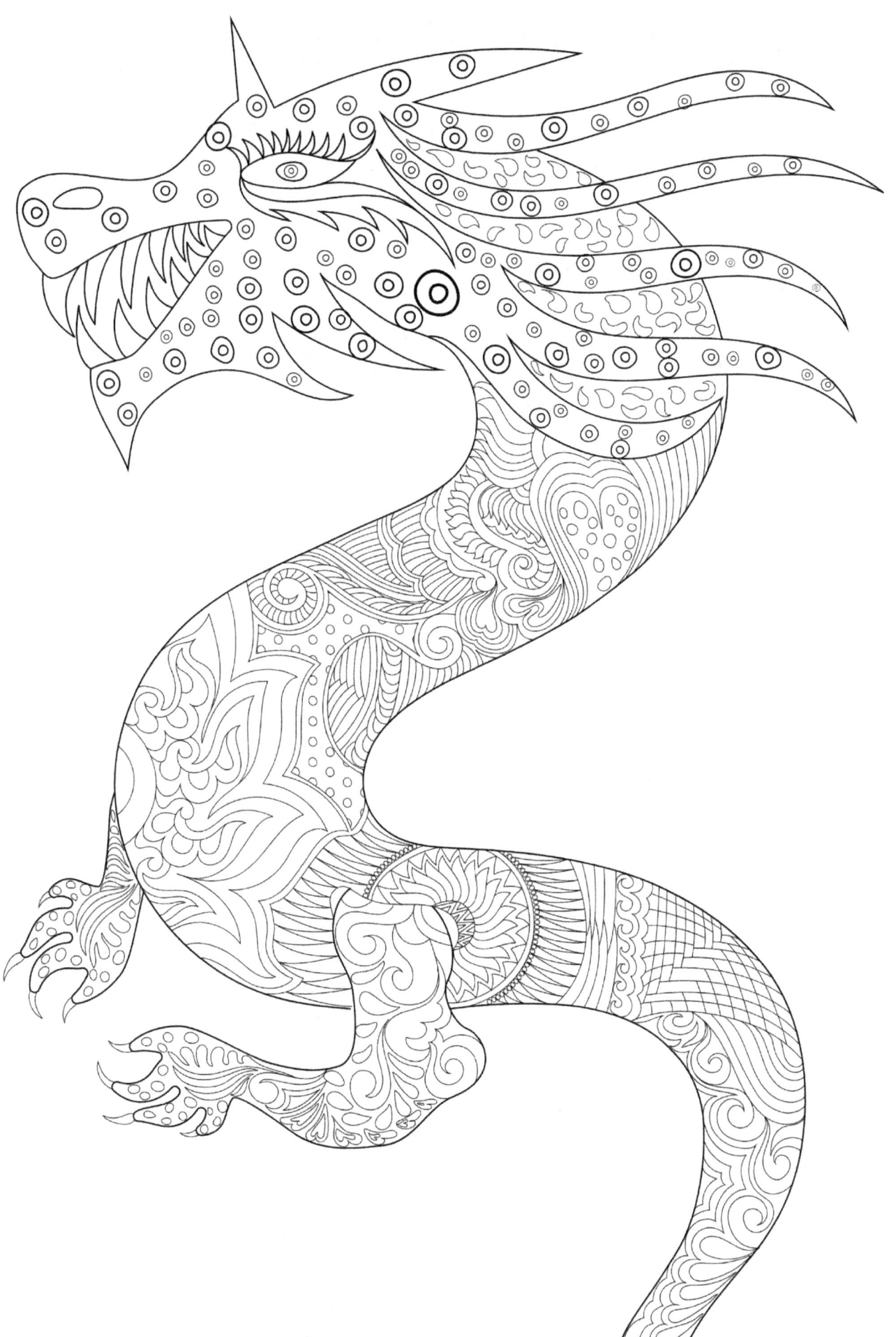

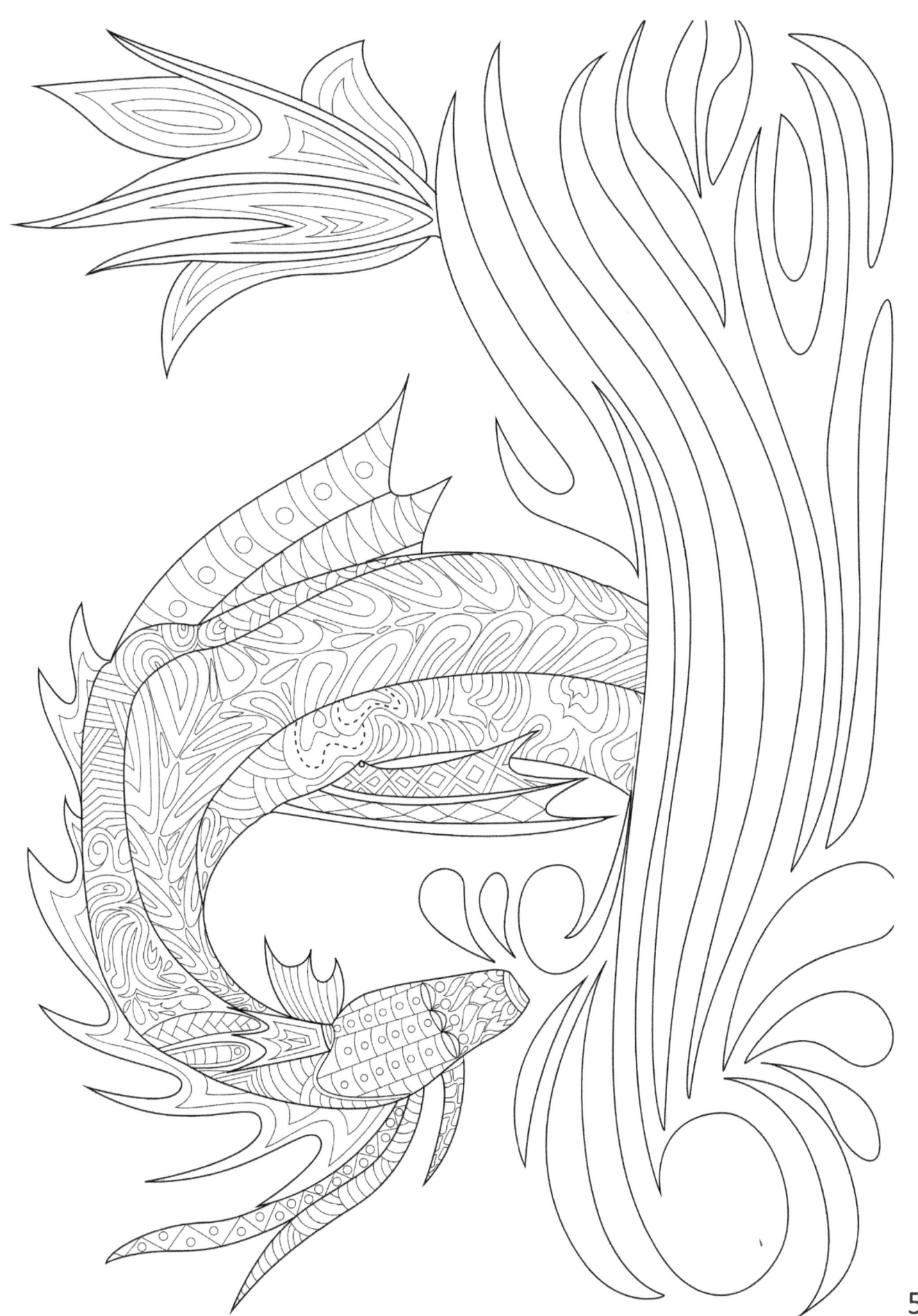

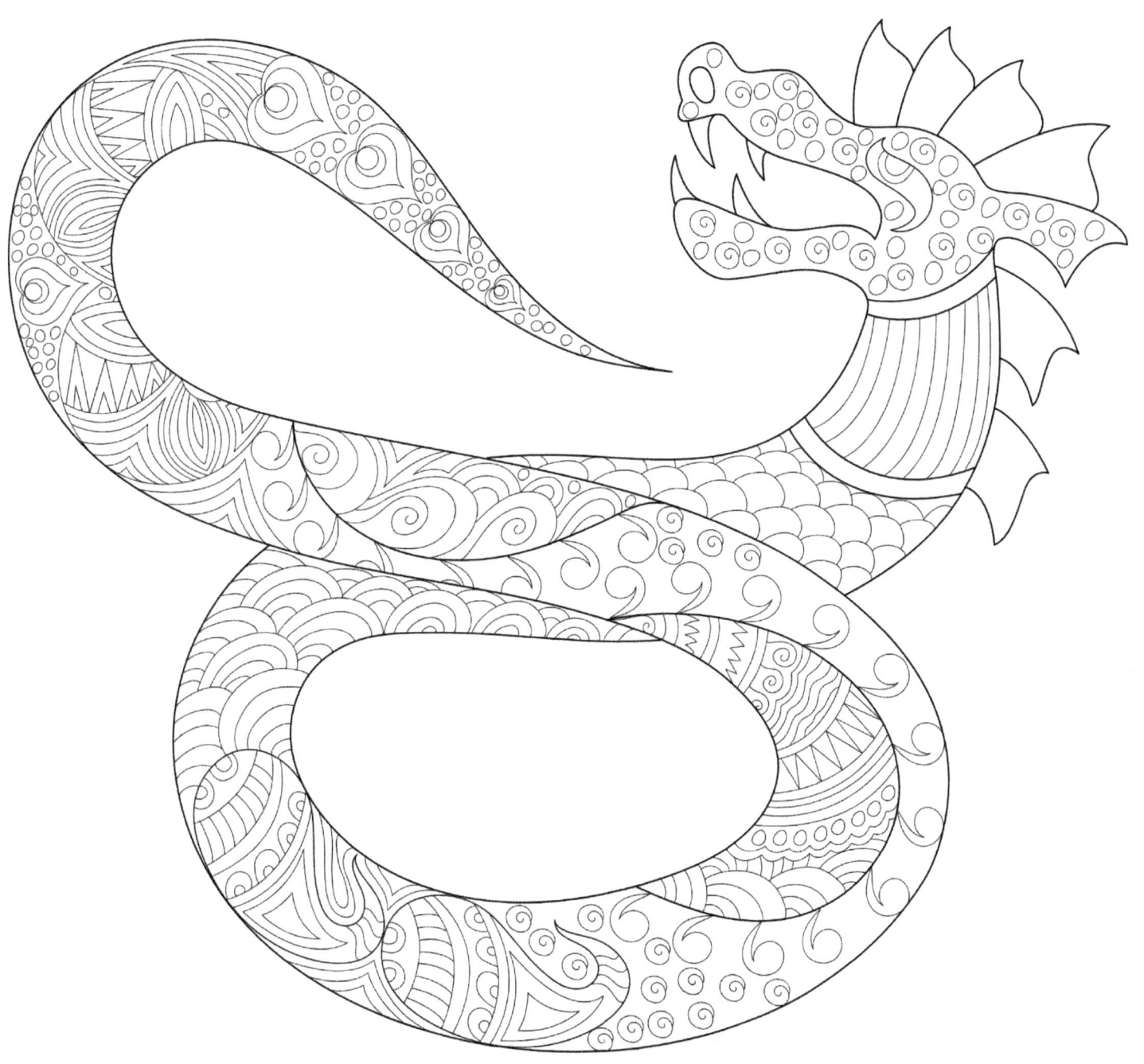

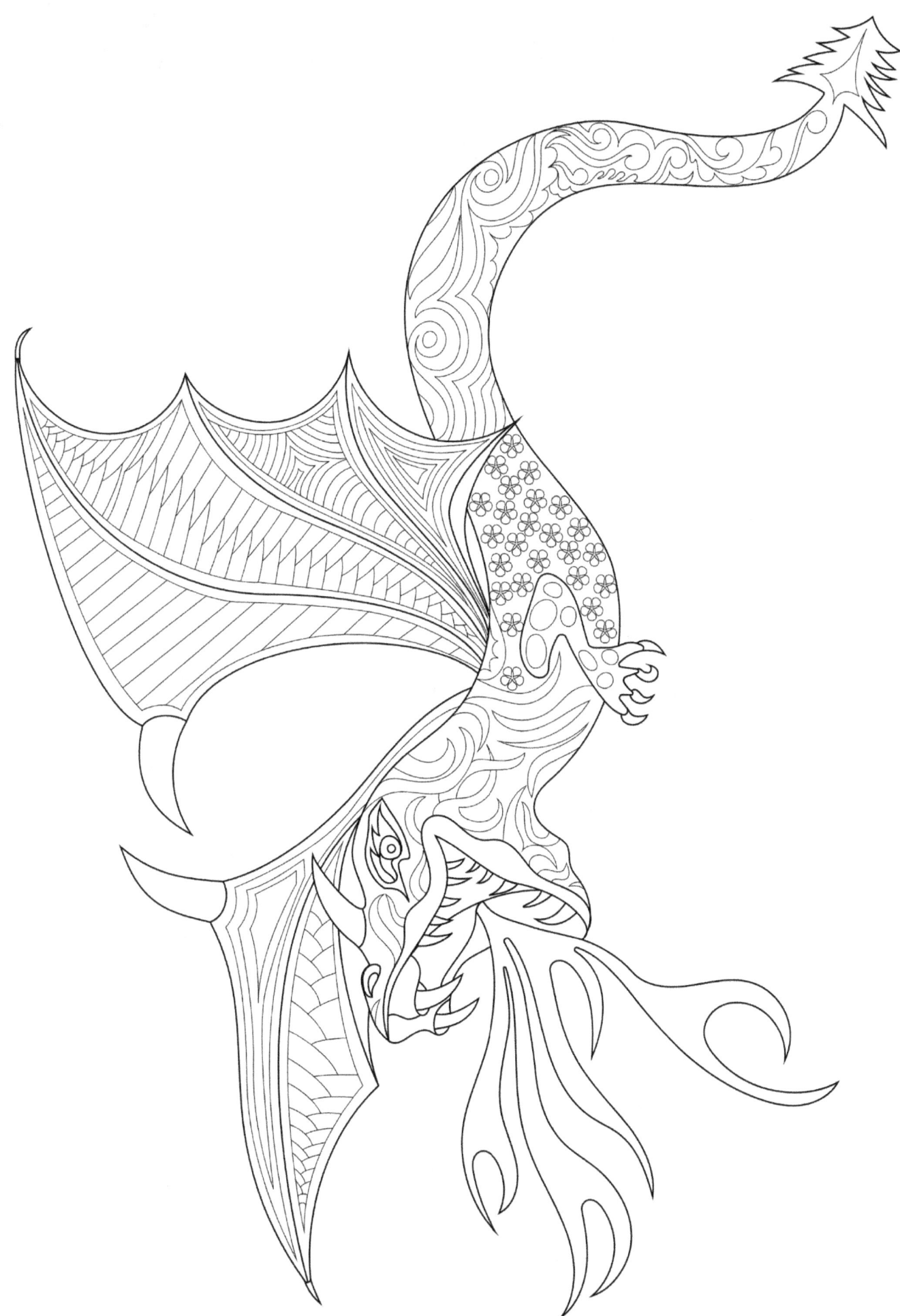

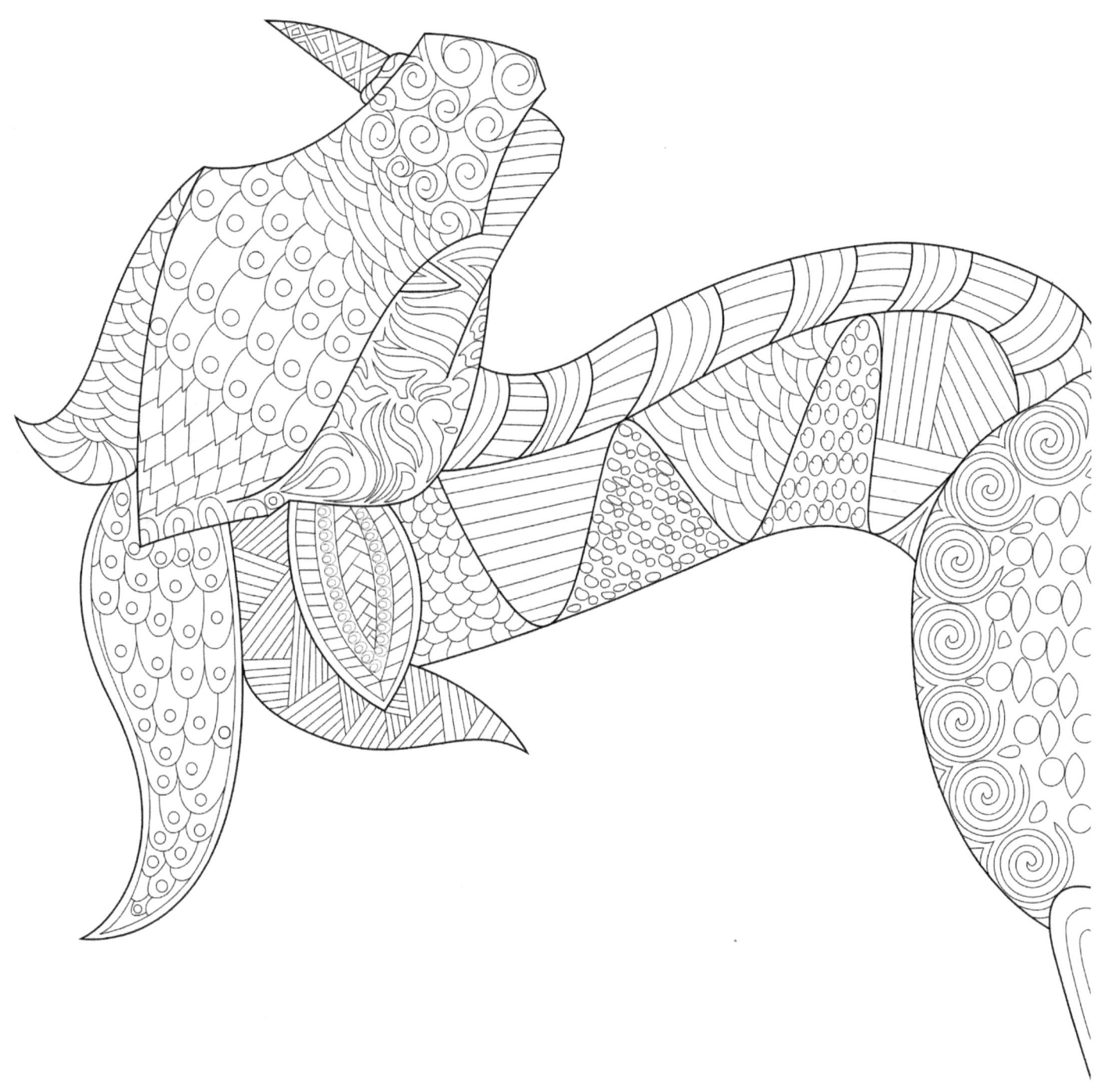

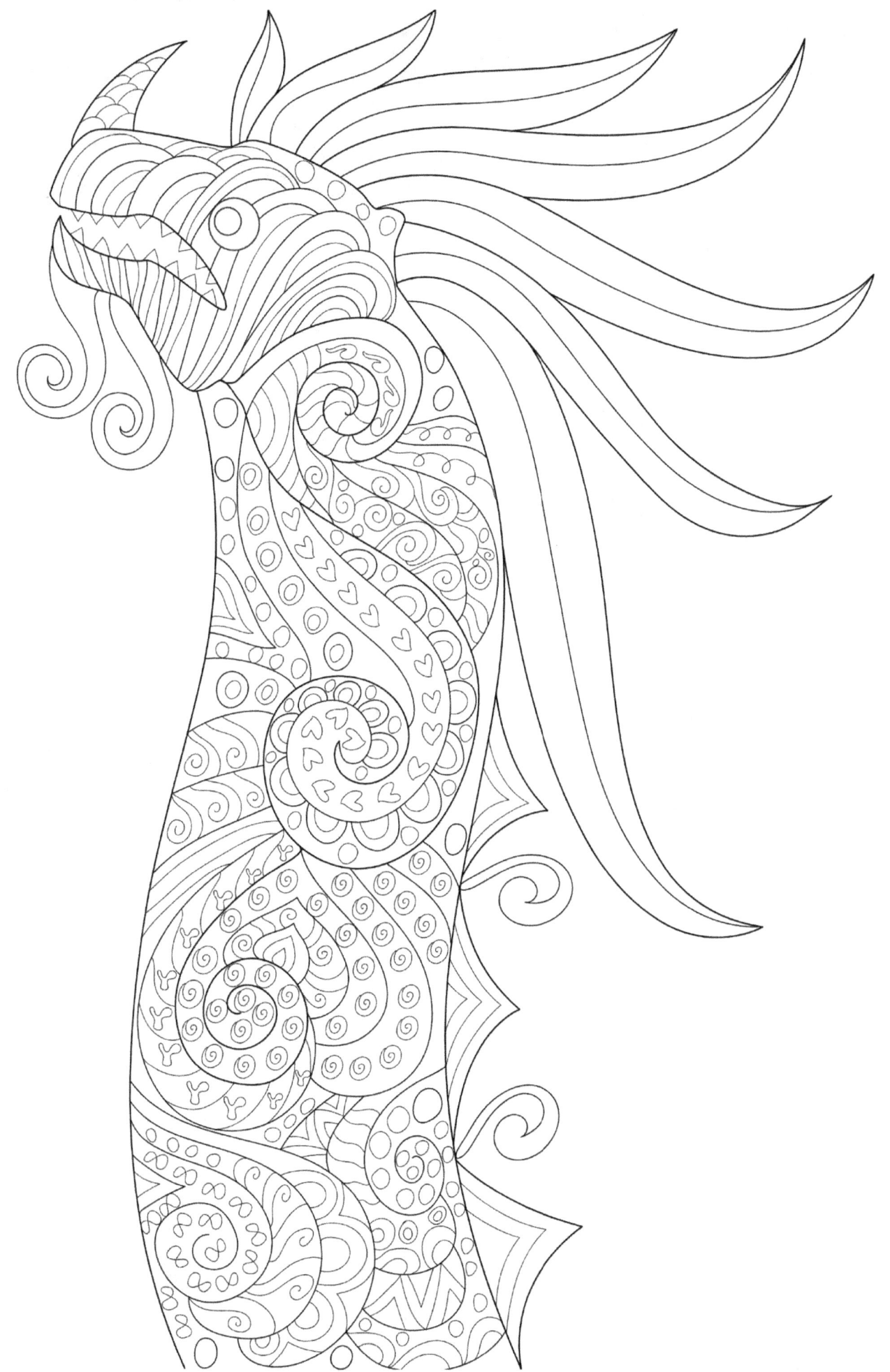

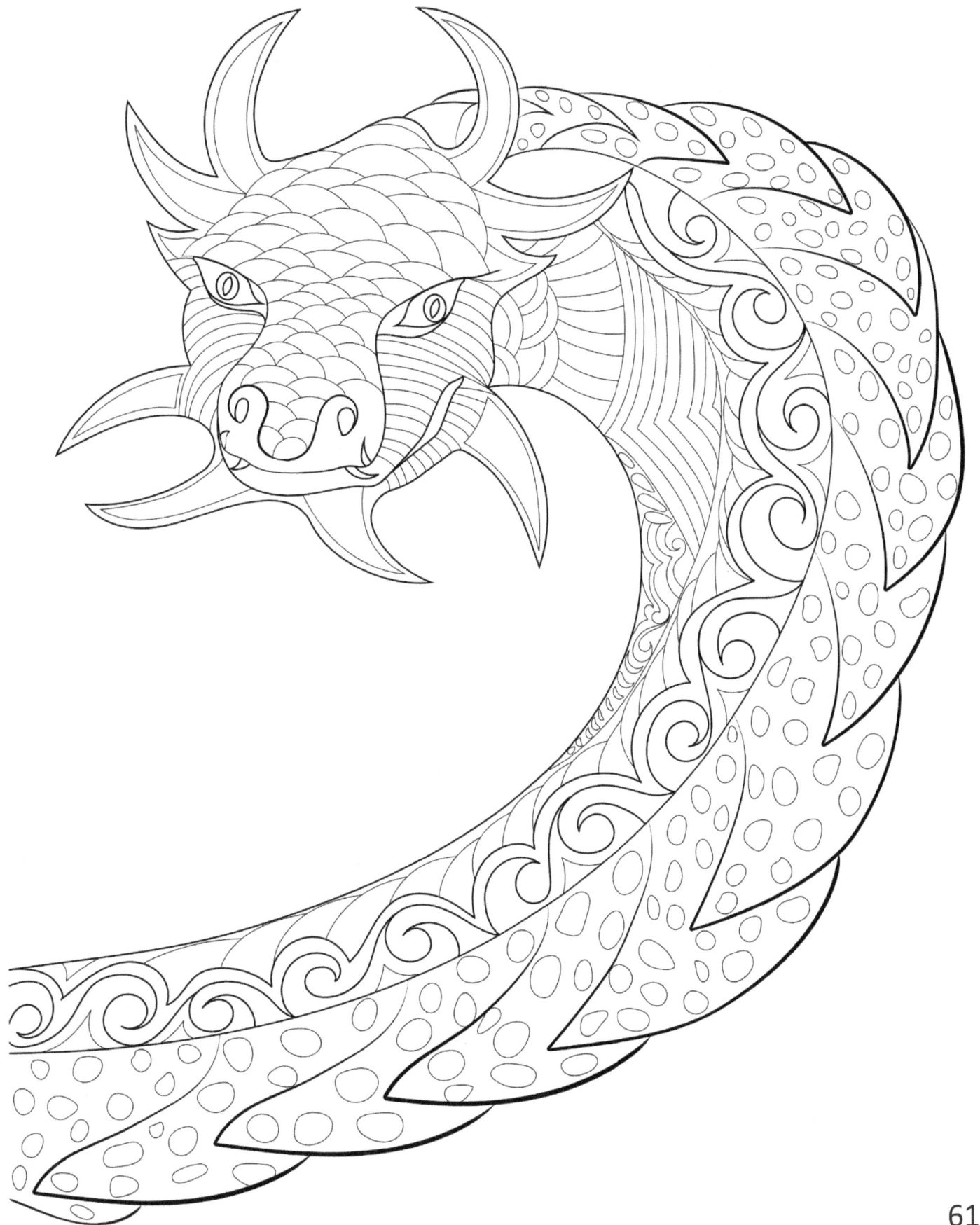

www.ingramcontent.com/pod-product-compliance
Lightning Source LLC
Chambersburg PA
CBHW080530220526
45465CB00006B/2659